CATALAN
Dictionary
&
Phrasebook

CATALAN
Dictionary
&
Phrasebook

A. Scott Britton

HIPPOCRENE BOOKS, INC.
New York

For information, address:
HIPPOCRENE BOOKS, INC.
171 Madison Avenue
New York, NY 10016
www.hippocrenebooks.com

Library of Congress Cataloging-in-Publication Data

Britton, A. Scott.
 Catalan dictionary and phrasebook / by A. Scott Britton.
      p. cm.
 English and Catalan.
 ISBN-13: 978-0-7818-1258-0 (pbk.)
 ISBN-10: 0-7818-1258-5 (pbk.)
 1. Catalan language--Dictionaries--English. 2. English
language--Dictionaries--Catalan. I. Title.
 PC3891.B75 2010
 449'.9321--dc22

                              2010010603

Printed in the United States of America.

CONTENTS

Introduction	vii
Abbreviations	ix
Catalan Pronunciation	1
Catalan Grammar	5
Catalan – English Dictionary	17
English – Catalan Dictionary	75
Phrasebook	135
Essential Phrases	137
Greetings & Basic Conversation	139
Exclamations & Interjections	142
Accommodations	145
Transportation	147
Directions	149
Food & Dining	151
Entertainment	157
People & Relationships	159
Clothing & Accessories	162
Colors	165
Technology	166
Medical	169

Parts of the Body	171
Hygiene	174
Weather	176
The Environment	177
Animals, Insects & Aquatic Life	179
Emergencies	182
Numbers	184
Time	189
Dates	193
Measures & Conversions	195
Appendix: 25 Catalan Verbs	197

INTRODUCTION

Catalan, or *català* to its speakers, is a member of the enormous Indo-European language group. Specifically, it is a Romance language, sharing a common linguistic history with French, Italian, Portuguese, and Spanish, to name but a few. Catalan is spoken by over seven million people in Catalonia on Spain's east coast and Mediterranean isles, in the Principality of Andorra (located in the Pyrenees mountain range between the French and Spanish borders), French Rousillion, and the city of Alghero on Italy's island of Sardinia. It is not, as many have assumed, a dialect of Spanish, but a distinct language unto itself. This misunderstanding is but one factor that has drawn speakers of Catalan to possess a fierce pride in their language, an attitude that is freely demonstrated and visible throughout the Catalan-speaking world. This, however, has not always been the case.

The Catalan language and culture experienced a long period of suppression once dictator Francisco Franco came to power in Spain in the late 1930s. Under Franco the Catalan language was limited significantly. The use of Catalan in government capacities was strictly forbidden, and the language was relegated mostly to personal use such as communication in the home. Franco did relax some of these limitations over time, but the complete freedom to use the Catalan language in any and all situations would only come after the ruler's demise. In the late 1970s, Catalonia was granted the status of Spanish autonomous region, which included the recognition of Catalan as the region's official language. Catalonia, its people, and its language have since grown to prominence not only in Spain but in all of Europe.

*   *   *

Readers who have had any experience with French or Spanish will recognize a significant degree of similarity to those languages in Catalan. Despite Catalan's close connections with other Romance languages, however, one need not possess an understanding of any of these to use this dictionary and phrasebook.

This book is geared toward users who need to converse in Catalan on a wide variety of subjects. These topics are thoroughly covered in the phrasebook portion of the book, ranging from typical sightseeing activities such as telling time and buying tickets for subway travel, to more serious matters like describing an ailment to a doctor. Further, the phrasebook portion is supplemented by an extensive two-way dictionary and primers on pronunciation and grammar, allowing readers to change and adjust given examples in order to fit their own precise, personalized needs. This dictionary and phrasebook will help the reader communicate in the most effective and efficient way possible, regardless of subject matter.

ABBREVIATIONS

abbr.	abbreviation
adj.	adjective
adv.	adverb
art.	article
conj.	conjunction
def.	definite
dem.	demonstrative
f.	feminine
fam.	familiar
form.	formal
indef.	indefinite
interj.	interjection
m.	masculine
n.	noun
num.	number
per.	person
pers.	personal
pl.	plural
pos.	possessive
prep.	preposition
pron.	pronoun
rel.	relative
sing.	singular
v.	verb

CATALAN PRONUNCIATION

Vowels

a
1. Stressed: as in *tall*
2. Unstressed: like final *a* in *banana*

e
1. Stressed: as in *met*
2. Stressed II: like long *a* in *make*
3. Unstressed: like second *e* in *telephone*

i
1. Stressed and unstressed: like *i* in *chlorine*
2. Unstressed and connecting two other vowels: like *y* in *yellow*
3. Silent when followed by *x*

o
1. Stressed: as in *slot*
2. Stressed II: like long *o* in *cone*
3. Unstressed: like double *o* in *moon*

u
1. Stressed and unstressed: like long *u* in *ruby*
2. Unstressed and connecting two other vowels: like *w* in *win*
3. Silent when following *g* or *q* and then followed by an *e* or *i*. This rule is negated, however, and *u* is pronounced like *w* when it is marked with a dieresis (*ü*). *U* following *g* or *q* and then itself followed by *a* or *o* is also pronounced like *w*. Examples: *guava*, *quick*.

Diphthongs & Triphthongs

In Catalan each vowel that occurs in a cluster of two or three is pronounced distinctly and separately from the other vowel(s) in the cluster. The rules discussed above for vowel pronunciation apply, too, with diphthongs and triphthongs.

Consonants

b   Like *b* in *best*

c   1. When followed by *e* or *i*, pronounced as in *center*
       2. Otherwise, pronounced as in *cat*

ç   Like *s* in *simple*

d   1. In the initial position or following *n*, *m*, or *l*, pronounced like *d* in *dinner*
       2. At the end of words, like *t* in *hut*
       3. In the interior of words and followed by a vowel, pronounced like *th* in *them*

f   Like *f* in *family*

g   1. When followed by *e* or *i*, pronounced like *s* in *pleasure*
       2. At the end of a word, pronounced like *k* in *kick*, except when the ending is *-aig*, *-eig*, *-oig*, *-uig*, or simply stressed *-ig* directly after a consonant, at which point it is pronounced like *-tch* in *pitch*
       3. In other instances, pronounced approximately like *g* in *gift*

h   Silent

j   Like *s* in *treasure*

k   Like English *k* (found only in loan words)

l	1. Like *l*, as in both *lamp* and *salt*
	2. Double *l* (*ll*) is pronounced like *y* in *yes*
	3. two *l*s separated by a dot (*l·l*) are pronounced separately in succession, as in *intel·ligent*
m	Like English *m*
n	Like English *n*, except before *f* or *v*, when it is pronounced roughly like English *m*
p	Like English *p*
q	*q* is always followed by *u*; pronounced like *q* in *quote*
r	1. Trilled in the initial position and when doubled
	2. Usually silent when at the end of a word
	3. Like English *r* in all other instances
s	Like English *s*, except when appearing between two vowels, when it is pronounced like English *z* (except in cases of double *s*, it reverts to standard English *s* pronunciation)
t	Usually like English *t*
v	Like English *b*, as in *tribute*
w	Like English *b* (found only in loan words)
x	1. At the beginning of a word and within a word and preceded by *i*, pronounced like English *sh*
	2. Pronounced like English *x* in *text* in most other situations
y	Like English *y*, as in *yard*
z	Like English *z*

Consonant Clusters

ll	Pronounced like *y* in *yes*
l·l	Indicates the separate pronunciation of each *l*, like in *inte<u>ll</u>igent*
ny	Pronounced like *ny* in *ca<u>ny</u>on*
rr	Trilled; no English counterpart

In addition to the discussion of pronunciation principles here, a brief reminder for the pronunciation of the most difficult and misunderstood sounds in the Catalan language is included at the bottom of every page.

These are:

ix	Pronounced like *sh* in **sh**out
ll	Sounds like *y* in *yes*
l·l	Each *l* is pronounced separately, like the *ll* in *hello*
ç	Like the *s* in **s**ell
j	Closest English approximation is the *s* in *vision*
v	Pronounced like *b* in **b**oat

CATALAN GRAMMAR

The following is a brief description of Catalan grammar. In conjunction with the rest of the book, this section will help readers communicate quickly and in a variety of situations, while at the same time acting as a reference for continued study.

NOUNS

Gender
Nouns in Catalan reflect gender; they are either masculine or feminine in nature. For example:

Masculine:	**el dit** finger
Feminine:	**la corbata** tie

Technically there is no neuter form, although there is a small set of nouns that simultaneously refer to both genders. For example:

gerent manager
dentista dentist

In these instances the manager or dentist can be either male or female. In this class of nouns the gender of the entity to which the noun refers can be specified through the definite or indefinite articles. For example:

el dentista the (male) dentist
la dentista the (female) dentist

Plurals

The rules for plural formation may seem difficult, but they are formulaic and therefore learnable. A little patience and a lot of practice with native speakers will eventually lead the reader to a greater understanding of the subtleties of the Catalan language.

Plurals are formed by some degree of alteration to the noun, frequently with the simple addition of -*s* at the end of the word (this change occurs when the word ends in a consonant or an unstressed vowel other than -*a*). For example:

> **diccionari** dictionary
> **diccionaris** dictionaries

Words ending in unstressed -*a* replace that letter with -*es* in the plural. For example:

> **paraula** word
> **paraules** words

When a word ends in a stressed vowel, replace that vowel with its unstressed form (that is, any accent mark appearing in the original word is omitted in the transformation) and add -*ns*. For example:

> **mà** hand
> **mans** hands

A fourth pattern exists to address a particular set of masculine nouns. Words ending with -ç, -*s*, or -*x*, or consonant clusters that produce an "s"-like sound (such as *-sc*, *-st*, and *-xt*) usually add *-os*. For example:

braç arm
braços arms

and

gust taste
gustos tastes

ARTICLES

Articles in Catalan always appear before the noun, and agree in gender and number with the noun they modify. The definite article (*the*) in Catalan is represented by:

el	masculine singular
els	masculine plural
la	feminine singular
les	feminine plural
l'	*el*, *els*, *la*, and *les* all become *l'* when the noun begins with a vowel or the letter *h* (a process known as *elision*)

The indefinite article (*a* or *an*) is represented by:

un	masculine singular
uns	masculine plural
una	feminine singular
unes	feminine plural

ADJECTIVES

The usual placement of adjectives in a Catalan phrase or sentence is after the noun that is modified (although one will encounter many exceptions to this if embarking on a more intensive course of study). For example:

gos <u>intel·ligent</u>   <u>intelligent</u> dog

Most adjectives reflect gender:

peix <u>estrany</u>   <u>strange</u> fish
pregunta <u>estranya</u>   <u>strange</u> question

Some adjectives maintain a neutral form regardless of the noun that they modify:

idea <u>freqüent</u>   <u>frequent</u> idea
oferiment <u>freqüent</u>   <u>frequent</u> offering

In this example *idea* is feminine and *oferiment* is masculine; the adjective that modifies both of them, *freqüent*, is neutral and maintains the same form when interacting with both feminine and masculine nouns.

Catalan adjectives also reflect number. The rules for forming the plural of adjectives are the same as those governing pluralization of nouns (see *Nouns*, above, for these rules). Examples:

Singular: **casa <u>grossa</u>**   <u>big</u> house
Plural: **cases <u>grosses</u>**   <u>big</u> houses

ADVERBS

Adverbs in Catalan exhibit the same variety as their English counterparts—they represent everything from location (*prop* 'near,' and *lluny* 'far,' for example) to time phrases (*ara* 'now,' and *demà* 'tomorrow').

Catalan also utilizes -*ment* adverbs, equivalent to adverbs in English that end in -ly. Several -*ment* adverbs are listed in the dictionary portion of this guide, but the user can also create them with a fair amount of ease. In order to do this, one simply needs to take an adjective and add the -*ment* ending to the feminine form of the adjective (if an adjective is neutral, that is, has no gender reflection, simply add -*ment* to that form). For example:

Adjective: **exòtic /-a** (exotic) + **-ment** =
Adverb: **exòticament** (exotically)

Adjective: **intel·ligent** (intelligent) + **-ment** =
Adverb: **intel·ligentment** (intelligently)

PRONOUNS

Two types of pronouns are discussed here—subject pronouns and object pronouns. The subject pronouns represent the agent that is performing an action, while object pronouns represent either the beneficiary of an action, or the entity to whom an action is performed.

Subject Pronouns

	Singular	*Plural*
1st per.	**jo** I	**nosaltres** we
2nd per.	**tu** you (*fam.*)	**vosaltres** you (*fam.*)
3rd per.	**ell** he	**ells** they (*m.*)
	ella she	**elles** they (*f.*)
	vostè you (*form.*)	**vostès** you (*form.*)

Subject pronouns appear before the verb, although they are usually omitted, leaving the conjugated verb to reflect the subject. While omission of the subject pronouns is the normal practice, they are used for certain stylistic purposes, such as emphasis. *Córrer* 'to run,' and *caminar* 'to walk' are used in the example below:

> *I* run, *you* walk.
> **Jo** corro, **tu** camines.

Object Pronouns

Object pronouns most often appear before the verb. However, there are some instances where these pronouns occur after the verb. This placement is most notable in the command form and after verbs in the infinitive form (see examples of object pronoun usage at the end of this section).

	Before Verb		**After Verb**	
Sing.				
1st per. me	em	m'	-me	'm
2nd per. you	et	t'	-te	't
3rd per. him	el, li*	l', li*	-lo, -li*	'l, -li*
her	la, li*	l', li*	-la, -li*	-la, -li*
it	ho	ho	-ho	-ho
Pl.				
1st per. us	ens	ens	-nos	'ns
2nd per. you	us	us	-vos	-us
3rd per. them (*m.*) els	els	-los	'ls
them (*f.*) les,	les,	-les,	-les,
els*	els*		-los*	'ls*

* In particle pairs marked with an asterisk the first particle represents the direct object pronoun (the action is performed on the object), while the second represents the indirect object pronoun (the object benefits from the action); all of those that are unmarked represent both direct object *and* indirect object pronouns, depending on the context in which they are used.

Examples of the use of object pronouns are numerous; what follows are a few representative instances:

Direct Object Examples:

He loves <u>her</u>.   **<u>L'</u>estima.**
<u>I</u> like shellfish.   **<u>M'</u>agrada el marisc.**
(*Lit.*: 'Shellfish pleases me.')

Indirect Object Examples:

I will buy <u>her</u> a coffee.   **<u>Li</u> compraré un cafè.**

They give <u>him</u> money.   **<u>Li</u> donen diners.**

Post-Verb Placement Examples— Command Form:

Help <u>me</u>!   **Ajudi'<u>m</u>!**
Listen to <u>them</u>!   **Escolti'<u>ls</u>!**

Post-Verb Placement Examples— Infinitives:

to bother <u>you</u>   **molestar-<u>te</u>**
to say <u>it</u>   **dir-<u>ho</u>**

VERBS

Catalan verbs fall into three classes: those that end in *-ar*, those that end in *-ir*, and those that end in *-er* (a fourth type, those that end in *-re*, are conjugated like the *-er* verbs). When verbs appear in these forms they are said to be unconjugated; this represents the infinitive form, the 'to …' portion of phrases like 'to run,' 'to eat,' or 'to be' in English. Verb conjugation usually consists of replacing these with new endings that reflect the particular tense or action that the speaker wants to express. For example:

Unconjugated (infinitive form):
    <u>to</u> sing   **cant<u>ar</u>**
Conjugated in the present tense:
    <u>I</u> sing   **cant<u>o</u>**

Conjugation Tables

Twenty-five essential, model verbs appear in the appendix of this book fully conjugated in the manner discussed below. Users can conjugate most Catalan verbs according to the patterns laid out in that section.

Tenses

Catalan verbs are expressed in fifteen different tenses. However, because effective, everyday communication doesn't necessarily call for the more complex forms, this book discusses only five of the most essential tenses.

1. **Present tense.** Indicates actions that transpire in the present.

   compra he or she buys

2. **Imperfect tense.** Used for past actions that occur over an indefinite time span.

   comprava he or she bought / was buying (*over an extended and unmeasured time span*)

3. **Preterite tense.** Indicates an action's occurrence once or in a measured time span.

   va comprar he or she bought (*a measured one-time event*)

4. **Future tense.** Indicates an action that will occur in the future.

   comprarà he or she will buy

5. **Imperative tense** (or command form).

    Compri! Buy!

Gerunds

Converting infinitive verbs into the gerund form (like English verbs that end with -ing) consists of replacing the *-ar*, *-ir*, or *-er/-re* endings with *-ant*, *-int*, and *-ent*, respectively. For example:

    have **tenir**
    hav<u>ing</u> **ten<u>int</u>**

A Note on the Dictionary Entries

In this dictionary most Catalan adjectives appear with an alternative ending, denoted by a slash (/). The first form listed is the masculine form, while the alternative ending represents the feminine variation of the word.
For example:

dull *adj.* avorrit /-ida

The reader must remove the masculine ending *-it* and replace it at the same spot (the letter *i* in this case acts as the place marker for the transformation) with the feminine ending *-ida*. There are a relatively small number of exceptions to this. Where masculine adjectives end in a vowel, replace the existing vowel with *a* in order to form the feminine. When the masculine form does not end with a vowel (and it is not a masculine adjective ending in *-it*, as discussed above), adding *a* will form the feminine in this case, too. For example:

exact *adj.* exacte /-a

Exacte is the masculine form of the adjective, while *exacta* is the feminine form.

mischievous *adj.* dolent /-a

Dolent is the masculine form of the adjective and *dolenta* is the feminine form.

CATALAN – ENGLISH
DICTIONARY

A

a *prep.* to, at
a través *prep.* across
a.C. *abbr.* B.C.
abandonar *v.* abandon
abans *adv.* before
abastar *v.* reach
abdomen *n.m.* abdomen
abella *n.f.* bee
abril *n.m.* April
absent *adj.* absent
absolutament *adv.* absolutely
acabat /-ada *adj.* (*finished*) over
acadèmia *n.f.* academy
accent *n.m.* accent
acceptar *v.* accept
accessori *n.m.* accessory
accident *n.m.* accident
acordar *v.* agree
acre *n.m.* acre
acte *n.m.* act
activitat *n.f.* activity
actor *n.m.* actor
actriu *n.f.* actress
actuar *v.* act
acumular *v.* gather
acurat /-ada *adj.* careful
adaptador *n.m.* adapter
addicional *adj.* additional
adéu *interj., n.m.* goodbye
adjectiu *n.m.* adjective
admetre *v.* admit
admirar *v.* admire
adoptar *v.* adopt
adreça *n.f.* address

ix = **sh**out, ll = **y**es, l·l = he**ll**o

adult /-a *adj., n.* adult
adverbi *n.m.* adverb
advocat /-ada *n.* attorney, lawyer
aeroport *n.m.* airport
afaitar *v.* shave
afecte *n.m.* affection
afegir *v.* add
afillada *n.f.* goddaughter
afillat *n.m.* godson
afortunat /-ada *adj.* lucky
agafar *v.* take, grab, catch
agitar *v.* stir
agost *n.m.* August
agradable *adj.* nice, pleasant
agrair *v.* thank
agre /-a *adj.* sour
agulla dels cabells *n.f.* hairpin
agut /-uda *adj.* sharp
ahir *adv.* yesterday
aigua *n.f.* water
aiguaneu *n.f.* sleet
aigüera *n.f.* sink
aire *n.m.* air
aire condicionat *n.m.* air conditioner
això *dem. pron.* this
ajudar *v.* help
ajustar *v.* adjust
ajut *n.m.* help
al costat *prep.* beside
al·lèrgia *n.f.* allergy
ala *n.f.* wing
alba *n.f.* dawn; daylight
albergínia *n.f.* eggplant
alçar-se *v.* stand (up)
alcohol *n.m.* alcohol
aleshores *adv.* then

ç = sell, j = vision, v = boat

alfabet *n.m.* alphabet
alga *n.f.* seaweed
àlgebra *n.f.* algebra
algú *pron.* someone, somebody; anybody, anyone
algun /-a *adj., pron.* some; any
aliança *n.f.* engagement ring; wedding ring
aliment *n.m.* food
all *n.m.* garlic
allà *adv.* there
allí *adv.* there
allò *dem. pron.* that
alt /-a *adj.* high, tall
altre /-a *adj.* other, another
AM *n.f.* a.m.
amable *adj.* kind
amagar *v.* hide
amanida *n.f.* salad
amant *n.* lover
amar *v.* love
amb *prep.* with
ambaixada *n.f.* embassy
ambdós /-dues *adj., pron.* both
ambient *n.m.* environment
ambulància *n.f.* ambulance
americà /-ana *adj., n.* American
ametlla *n.f.* almond
amic /-iga *n.* friend
amor *n.m.* love
ample /-a *adj.* wide
ampolla *n.f.* bottle
anar *v.* go
anarquia *n.f.* anarchy
anarquista *n.* anarchist
ànec *n.m.* duck
anell *n.m.* ring

ix = **sh**out, ll = **y**es, l·l = he**ll**o

anèmia *n.f.* anemia
àngel *n.m.* angel
angle *n.m.* angle
anglès[1] *n.m.* English language
anglès[2] **/-esa** *adj., n.* English
anguila *n.f.* eel
ànima *n.f.* soul
animal *n.m.* animal
anit *adv.* last night
aniversari *n.m.* anniversary; birthday
anomenar *v.* name
antibiòtic *n.m.* antibiotic
antic /-iga *adj.* ancient
antiguitat *n.f.* antique
anunci *n.m.* advertisement
anunciar *v.* announce, advertise
any *n.m.* year
any bixest *n.m.* leap year
anyil *n.m.* indigo
apagat /-ada *adj.* off
aparcar *v.* park
aparèixer *v.* appear
aparell *n.m.* appliance
àpat *n.m.* meal
aperitiu *n.m.* appetizer
api *n.m.* celery
aplaudir *v.* applaud
aprendre *v.* learn
aprovar *v.* approve
apunyalar *v.* stab
aquell *dem. adj.* (*far*) that
aquella *dem. adj.* (*far*) that
aquelles *dem. adj., pron.* (*far*) those
aquells *dem. adj., pron.* (*far*) those
aquest *dem. adj.* this, (*near*) that
aquesta *dem. adj.* this, (*near*) that

ç = sell, j = vision, v = boat

aquesta nit *adv.* tonight
aquestes *dem. adj., pron.* these, (*near*) those
aquests *dem. adj., pron.* these, (*near*) those
aquí *adv.* here
ara *adv.* now
aranya *n.f.* spider
arbre *n.m.* tree
arbust *n.m.* bush
arc de Sant Martí *n.m.* rainbow
àrea *n.f.* area
arena *n.f.* arena
argüir *v.* argue
àrid /-a *adj.* dry
arna *n.f.* moth
arracada *n.f.* earring
arrel *n.f.* root
arrestar *v.* arrest
arribada *n.f.* arrival
arribar *v.* arrive, (*~ a destination*) reach
arròs *n.m.* rice
art *n.m.* art
artell *n.m.* knuckle
artificial *adj.* artificial
artista *n.* artist
artritis *n.f.* arthritis
ascensor *n.m.* elevator
ase *n.m.* donkey
asma *n.f.* asthma
asolellat /-ada *adj.* sunny
assecador *n.m.* hair dryer
assecadora *n.f.* clothes dryer
assecar *v.* dry
assegurança de cotxes *n.f.* car insurance
assistir *v.* attend
associació *n.f.* association
atac *n.m.* attack

ix = **sh**out, ll = **y**es, l·l = he**ll**o

atacar *v.* attack
ataronjat /-ada *adj.* (*color*) orange
atenció *n.f.* attention
aterratge *n.m.* landing
Atlàntic *n.m.* Atlantic
atlas *n.m.* atlas
atmosfera *n.f.* atmosphere
attreure *v.* attract
australià /-ana *adj., n.* Australian
autobús *n.m.* bus
automàtic *adj.* automatic
autor *n.* author
auxiliar de vol *n.* flight attendant
avall *adv.* down
avantpassat *n.m.* ancestor
avi *n.m.* grandfather
àvia *n.f.* grandmother
aviat *adv.* soon
avinguda *n.f.* avenue
avió *n.m.* airplane
aviram *n.f.* poultry
avis *n.m.* grandparents
avís *n.m.* warning
avisar *v.* warn
avorrit /-ida *adj.* boring, dull
avui *adv.* today

B

bacallà *n.m.* cod fish
badia *n.f.* bay
baia *n.f.* berry
baix /-a *adj.* low
balena *n.f.* whale
ball *n.m.* dance
ballar *v.* dance

ç = sell, j = vision, v = **b**oat

banana *n.f.* banana
banc *n.m.* bank
bandera *n.f.* flag
bany *n.m.* restroom, bathroom; toilet; bath
banyar-se *v.* bathe
banyera *n.f.* bathtub
barat /-a *adj.* cheap, inexpensive
barba *n.f.* beard
barbacoa *n.f.* barbecue
barbeta *n.f.* chin
barca *n.f.* boat
barcassa *n.f.* barge
barnús *n.m.* bathrobe
barret *n.m.* hat
bàsic /-a *adj.* basic
bàsquet *n.m.* basketball
bassa *n.f.* pond
bata *n.f.* gown
bateria *n.f.* battery
be *n.m.* sheep, lamb
bé *adj., adv.* well
beguda *n.f.* drink, beverage
beisbol *n.m.* baseball
bell /-a *adj.* beautiful, handsome
bellesa *n.f.* beauty
benvingut /-uda *interj.* welcome
bes *n.m.* kiss
besar *v.* kiss
bestiar boví *n.m.* cattle
beure *v.* drink
bicicleta *n.f.* bicycle
bistec *n.m.* steak
bitllet *n.m.* ticket
blanc /-a *adj.* white
blat *n.m.* wheat
blat de moro *n.m.* corn

ix = **sh**out, ll = **y**es, l·l = he**ll**o

blau /-ava *adj.* blue
bo /-ona *adj.* good
boca *n.f.* mouth
boira *n.f.* fog
boirós /-osa *adj.* foggy
bol *n.m.* bowl
boleivol *n.m.* volleyball
bolet *n.m.* mushroom
bolígraf *n.m.* pen
bonic /-a *adj.* pretty (*f.*), beautiful (*f.*), handsome (*m.*)
bosc *n.m.* forest, woods
bossa *n.f.* bag; purse
bot salvavides *n.m.* lifeboat
botes *n.f.* boots
botiga *n.f.* store, shop
botó *n.m.* button
boxa *n.f.* boxing
braç *n.m.* arm
braçalet *n.m.* bracelet
brillant *adj.* bright
brisa *n.f.* breeze
broma *n.f.* joke; fun
bromós /-osa *adj.* hazy
bròquil *n.m.* broccoli
brou *n.m.* broth
brúixola *n.f.* compass
brusa *n.f.* blouse
brut /-a *adj.* dirty
brutícia *n.f.* dirt
bufar *v.* blow
buit /-ida *adj.* empty
bullir *v.* boil
buscar *v.* look for, seek, search
butxaca *n.f.* pocket

ç = sell, j = vision, v = boat

C

cabina *n.f.* cabin
cable *n.m.* cable
cabra *n.f.* goat
caçar *v.* hunt
cacauet *n.m.* peanut
cada *adj.* each
cadira *n.f.* chair
cafè *n.m.* coffee; café
cafetera *n.f.* coffee pot
caiguda *n.f.* fall
caiman *n.m.* alligator
caixa *n.f.* box
caixa forta *n.f.* safe
caixer automàtic *n.m.* ATM
calamar *n.m.* squid
calamarsa *n.f.* hail
calamarsejar *v.* hail
calculadora *n.f.* calculator
calendari *n.m.* calendar
calent /-a *adj.* hot, warm
calma *adj.* calm
calor *n.f.* heat
cama *n.f.* leg
cambra *n.f.* room
cambrer /-a *n.* waiter (*m.*), waitress (*f.*),
   server
càmera *n.f.* camera
càmera de vídeo *n.f.* video camera
camí *n.m.* path, road
caminar *v.* walk; step
camió *n.m.* truck
camisa *n.f.* shirt
camp *n.m.* field
camp de golf *n.m.* golf course

ix = **sh**out, ll = **y**es, l·l = he**ll**o

campana *n.f.* bell
canadenc /-a *adj., n.* Canadian
canari *n.m.* canary
cancel·lar *v.* cancel
cançó *n.f.* song
canell *n.m.* wrist
canoa *n.f.* canoe
cansalada *n.f.* bacon
cansat /-ada *adj.* tired
cantar *v.* sing
cantó *n.m.* corner
canviar *v.* change; exchange
canya *n.f.* shin
canyella *n.f.* cinnamon
canyó *n.m.* canyon
cap *n.m.* top; head
cap a *prep.* toward
cap al mar *adv.* seaward
cap amunt *adv.* upward
cap d'any *n.m.* New Year's Eve
cap de setmana *n.m.* weekend
capacitat *n.f.* ability
capità *n.m.* captain
capsa *n.f.* box
capvespre *n.m.* dusk
car /-a *adj.* expensive
cara *n.f.* face
carabassa *n.f.* squash
caramel *n.m.* candy
carbassa *n.f.* pumpkin
carbassó *n.m.* zucchini
cargol *n.m.* snail
carlinga *n.f.* cockpit
carn *n.f.* meat, beef; flesh
carn de vedella *n.f.* veal
carnet de conduir *n.m.* driver's license

ç = **s**ell, j = vi**s**ion, v = **b**oat

càrrega *n.f.* cargo
carrer *n.m.* street
carreró *n.m.* alley
carretera *n.f.* road, highway
carril *n.m.* track
carta *n.f.* (*postal*) letter
cartera *n.f.* wallet
carxofa *n.f.* artichoke
casa *n.f.* house, home
casament *n.m.* marriage; wedding
casar-se *v.* marry
casat /-ada *adj.* married
cascada *n.f.* waterfall
cassó *n.m.* pan
cassola *n.f.* pan
castanya *n.f.* chestnut
castell *n.m.* castle
castellà *n.m.* Spanish language
català *n.m.* Catalan language
català /-ana *adj., n.* Catalan
catedral *n.f.* cathedral
catifa *n.f.* carpet
catòlic /-a *adj., n.* Catholic
catorze *num.* fourteen
caure *v.* fall
cava *n.m.* cava, champagne
cavalcar *v.* ride
cavall *n.m.* horse
cavall de mar *n.m.* seahorse
cavar *v.* dig
caverna *n.f.* cave
CD *n.m.* CD
ceba *n.f.* onion
cec /-ega *adj.* blind
cel *n.m.* sky
celebració *n.f.* celebration

ix = **sh**out, ll = **y**es, l·l = **h**ello

celebrar *v.* celebrate
cella *n.f.* eyebrow
Celsius *n.m.* Celsius
cementiri *n.m.* cemetery
cendra *n.f.* ash
cent *num.* hundred
centímetre *n.m.* centimeter
central *adj.* central
centre *n.m.* center
centre comercial *n.m.* shopping center, mall
cercle *n.m.* circle, ring
cert /-a *adj.* true; sure, certain
certament *adv.* certainly
cervell *n.m.* brain
cervesa *n.f.* beer
cérvol *n.m.* deer
cibercafè *n.m.* Internet café
cicatriu *n.f.* scar
ciència *n.f.* science
cigala *n.f.* locust
cigar *n.m.* cigar
cigarret *n.m.* cigarette
cim *n.m.* summit, peak
ciment *n.m.* cement
cinc *num.* five
cinema *n.m.* movie theater
cingle *n.m.* cliff
cinquanta *num.* fifty
cintura *n.f.* waist
cinturó *n.m.* belt
cinturó de seguretat *n.m.* seatbelt
cinturó salvavides *n.m.* life preserver
circ *n.m.* circus
cirera *n.f.* cherry
cirurgia *n.f.* surgery
cita *n.f.* appointment, date

ç = sell, j = vision, v = boat

ciutadà *n.m.* citizen
ciutat *n.f.* city, town
civada *n.f.* oat
clar /-a *adj.* clear; light
classe *n.f.* class
clau *n.f.* key
clínica *n.f.* clinic
cloïssa *n.f.* clam
closca *n.f.* shell
coberta *n.f.* cover
cobrir *v.* cover
coco *n.m.* coconut
cocodril *n.m.* crocodile
còctel *n.m.* cocktail
còdol *n.m.* pebble
cognom *n.m.* surname
coixí *n.m.* pillow
col *n.f.* cabbage
col·legi *n.m.* college
coll *n.m.* collar; neck
collaret *n.m.* necklace
collir *v.* (*pluck*) pick
còlon *n.m.* colon
colònia *n.f.* cologne
color *n.m.* color
coloret *n.m.* (*makeup*) blush
colze *n.m.* elbow
com *adv.* as, like; how
coma *n.f.* comma
combinació *n.f.* (*clothing*) slip
combinar *v.* combine
comèdia *n.f.* comedy
començar *v.* start, begin
còmode /-a *adj.* comfortable
companyia *n.f.* company
complet /-a *adj.* complete

ix = **sh**out, ll = **y**es, l·l = he**ll**o

completament *adv.* entirely
comprar *v.* buy
comprendre *v.* understand
comptar *v.* count
comú /-una *adj.* common
comunicar *v.* communicate
concert *n.m.* concert
condiment *n.m.* condiment
conductor *n.m.* driver
conduir *v.* drive
coneixement *n.m.* knowledge
conèixer *v.* know, be acquainted with
confessar *v.* admit
congelador *n.m.* freezer
congelar *v.* freeze
congratular *v.* congratulate
conill *n.m.* rabbit
connectar *v.* connect
consell *n.m.* advice
conseqüència *n.f.* result
conservar *v.* preserve
consonant *n.f.* consonant
constipat *n.m.* (*illness*) cold
construir *v.* build
conte *n.m.* story
contenidor *n.m.* container
contestador automàtic *n.m.* answering
　　machine
contestar *v.* answer
continent *n.m.* continent
continu /-ínua *adj.* constant
continuament *adv.* continually
continuar *v.* continue
contra *prep.* against
control remot *n.m.* remote control
controlar *v.* control

ç = sell, j = vision, v = boat

conversar *v.* talk
conyac *n.m.* brandy
copejar *v.* beat
copiar *v.* copy
copilot *n.m.* co-pilot
cor *n.m.* heart
corbata *n.f.* tie
cordill *n.m.* cord
corn *n.m.* horn
correcte /-a *adj.* correct
corredor *n.m.* aisle
corregir *v.* correct
corrent *n.m.* stream
córrer *v.* run
correu *n.m.* mail
correu de veu *n.m.* voicemail
correu electrònic *n.m.* e-mail
cos *n.m.* body
cosa *n.f.* thing
cosí /-ina *n.* cousin
cosir *v.* sew
cost *n.m.* cost
costa *n.f.* coast, seashore, shore
costar *v.* cost
costat *n.m.* side
costella de porc *n.f.* pork chop
cotxe *n.m.* car
coure *v.* cook, bake
cranc *n.m.* crab
cràter *n.m.* crater
crear *v.* create
créixer *v.* grow
crema *n.f.* cream; custard
cremallera *n.f.* zipper
cremar *v.* burn
creu *n.f.* cross

creure *v.* believe
criada *n.m.* maid
crida *n.f.* call
cridar *v.* scream, shout, yell, cry (out), call (out)
cristià /-ana *adj., n.* Christian
crit *n.m.* scream
cru /-a *adj.* raw
cua *n.f.* tail
cuart *n.m.* quart
cuc *n.m.* worm
cuca de llum *n.f.* firefly
cuina *n.f.* kitchen
cuir *n.m.* leather
cuixa *n.f.* thigh
cullera *n.f.* spoon
cultura *n.f.* culture
cunyada *n.f.* sister-in-law
cunyat *n.m.* brother-in-law
cursa de braus *n.f.* bullfight
cursor *n.m.* cursor
curt /-a *adj.* short

D

d.C. *abbr.* A.D.
d'acord *interj.* okay
dalt *adv.* up
damunt *adv.* over, above
d'anada *adj.* one-way
d'anada i tornada *adj.* round-trip
darrera *adv.* behind
data *n.f.* date
davant *adv.* ahead
de *prep.* of, from
de plata *adj.* silver

ç = sell, j = vision, v = boat

de qui *pos. pron.* whose
de vegades *adv.* sometimes
dèbil *adj.* weak
decidir *v.* decide
defensar *v.* defend
definició *n.f.* definition
definir *v.* define
deixar *v.* leave
delicat /-ada *adj.* delicate
deliciós /-osa *adj.* delicious
demà *adv.* tomorrow
demanar *v.* request
demostració *n.f.* demonstration
demostrar *v.* demonstrate
dent *n.f.* tooth
dentista *n.* dentist
des de *prep.* since
desagradable *adj.* unpleasant
desaparèixer *v.* disappear
descendent *adj.* downward
descriure *v.* describe
desembre *n.m.* December
desert *n.m.* desert
desfer *v.* undo
desig *n.m.* desire
desil·lusió *n.f.* disappointment
desitjar *v.* desire
desodorant *n.m.* deodorant
despertador *n.m.* alarm clock
despertar *v.* awaken
després *adv.* after; later
despullar *v.* undress
dessota *adv.* under
destituir *v.* dismiss (from somewhere)
destruir *v.* destroy
detall *n.m.* detail

ix = **sh**out, ll = **y**es, l·l = he**ll**o

deu *num.* ten
déu *n.m.* god
deure *n.m.* duty; *v.* owe
deute *n.m.* debt
devora *adv.* near
d'hora *adj.* early
dia *n.m.* day; daytime
dia de festa *n.m.* holiday
diabetis *n.f.* diabetes
dialecte *n.m.* dialect
diamant *n.m.* diamond
dic *n.m.* dam; dock, pier
diccionari *n.m.* dictionary
diferent *adj.* different
difícil *adj.* difficult; awkward
digital *adj.* digital
dijous *n.m.* Thursday
dilluns *n.m.* Monday
dimarts *n.m.* Tuesday
dimecres *n.m.* Wednesday
dinar *n.m.* lunch
diners *n.m.* money
dinou *num.* nineteen
dipòsit *n.m.* deposit
dipositar *v.* deposit
dir *v.* say, tell
direcció *n.f.* direction
director *n.m.* manager
disc dur *n.m.* hard drive
disculpa *n.f.* apology
disculpar-se *v.* apologize
disponible *adj.* available
disputa *n.f.* argument
dissabte *n.m.* Saturday
disset *num.* seventeen
distància *n.f.* distance

ç = sell, j = vision, v = **b**oat

districte *n.m.* district
dit *n.m.* finger
dit del peu *n.m.* toe
dita *n.f.* saying
diumenge *n.m.* Sunday
divendres *n.m.* Friday
divertir-se *v.* have fun
dividir *v.* divide
divuit *num.* eighteen
dofí *n.m.* dolphin
dòlar *n.m.* dollar
dolç[1] *n.m.* candy
dolç[2] **/-a** *adj.* sweet
dolent /-a *adj.* bad; mischievous
dolor *n.m.* pain, ache
dolorit /-ida *adj.* sore
dolorós /-osa *adj.* painful
dona *n.f.* woman
donar *v.* give
donar la benvinguda *v.* welcome
d'or *adj.* gold
dormida *n.f.* sleep
dormir *v.* sleep
dormitori *n.m.* bedroom
dos *num.* two
dos cops *adv.* twice
dotze *num.* twelve
dotzena *n.f.* dozen
dret /-a *adj.* right
droga *n.f.* drug
dubtar *v.* doubt
dubte *n.m.* doubt
dues *num.* two
dur /-a *adj.* hard
durant *prep.* during
dutxa *n.f.* shower

dutxar-se *v.* shower
DVD *n.m.* DVD

E

economia *n.f.* economy
edat *n.f.* age
edifici *n.m.* building
efecte *n.m.* effect
eixugar *v.* wipe
el *def. art.* the
elecció *n.f.* election
elèctric /-a *adj.* electric
electricitat *n.f.* electricity
elegir *v.* elect
elevar *v.* raise
ell *pron.* he
ella *pron.* she
elles *pron.* they
ells *pron.* they
els *pron.* them; *def. art.* the (*pl.*)
embarassada *adj.* pregnant
embarcar *v.* board
embenat *n.m.* bandage
emergència *n.f.* emergency
emoció *n.f.* emotion
empanada *n.f.* pie
empènyer *v.* push
en *prep.* in, on; at
encantador /-a *adj.* charming
encara *adv.* still
enciam *n.m.* lettuce
endarrera *adv.* back; backwards
enfadat /-ada *adj.* angry, mad
enfonsar-se *v.* sink
engolir *v.* swallow

ç = sell, j = vision, v = boat

enigma *n.m.* puzzle
enllestit /-ida *adj.* ready
enmig *adv.* between
ennuvolat /-ada *adj.* cloudy
enrojolar-se *v.* blush
ensenyar *v.* teach
entendre *v.* understand
enter /-a *adj.* entire
enterrar *v.* bury
entorn *adv.* around
entrada *n.f.* entrance
entranyes *n.f.* entrails
entrar *v.* enter
entre *prep.* between, among
entrenar *v.* train
entrepà *n.m.* sandwich
envers *prep.* toward
enviar *v.* send
envol *n.m.* take-off
equipatge *n.m.* luggage, baggage
error *n.m.* error, mistake
eruga *n.f.* caterpillar
esbandida bucal *n.f.* mouthwash
esbojarrat /-ada *adj.* crazy, mad
escalfador *n.m.* heater
escarabat *n.m.* beetle; cockroach
escocès /-esa *adj., n.* Scottish
escola *n.f.* school
escollir *v.* pick, choose
escoltar *v.* listen
escopir *v.* spit
escorça *n.f.* bark
escriure *v.* write
esdeveniment *n.m.* event
esdevenir *v.* become
esforç *n.m.* effort

ix = **sh**out, ll = **y**es, l·l = he**ll**o

església *n.f.* church
esmorzar *n.m.* breakfast
espantar *v.* scare
espantat /-ada *adj.* frightened
espanyol /-a *adj., n.* Spanish
espatlla *n.f.* shoulder
espècia *n.f.* spice
espectacle *n.m.* show
espelma *n.f.* candle
esperar *v.* wait; expect
esperit *n.m.* spirit
espès /-essa *adj.* thick
espòs *n.m.* husband
esposa *n.f.* wife
esquena *n.f.* back
esquerre /-ra *adj.* left
esquirol *n.m.* squirrel
ésser *v.* be (*for permanent qualities*)
est *n.m.* east
estació *n.f.* station; season
estació d'autobús *n.f.* bus station
estació de metro *n.f.* metro station, subway station
estació de tren *n.f.* train station
estadi *n.m.* stadium
estafeta *n.f.* post office
estar *v.* be (*for temporary qualities*)
estat *n.m.* state
estàtua *n.f.* statue
esternudar *v.* sneeze
estil *n.m.* style
estirar *v.* pull, stretch
estiu *n.m.* summer
estómac *n.m.* stomach
estovalles *n.f.* tablecloth
estranger /-a *adj.* foreign

ç = sell, j = vision, v = boat

estrany /-a *adj.* strange
estrella *n.f.* star
estrella de mar *n.f.* starfish
estret /-a *adj.* narrow
estudiant *n.m.* student
estufa *n.f.* stove
evitar *v.* avoid
exactament *adv.* exactly
exacte /-a *adj.* exact
examen *n.m.* exam
excel·lent *adj.* excellent
excitat *adj.* excited
excursió *n.f.* excursion
exemple *n.m.* example
experiència *n.f.* experience
explicar *v.* explain

F

fabricar *v.* (*create*) make
façana *n.f.* front
fàcil *adj.* easy
factura *n.f.* bill
facturar *v.* check
Fahrenheit *n.m.* Fahrenheit
faldilla *n.f.* skirt
fals /-a *adj.* wrong
família *n.f.* family
famós /-osa *adj.* famous
fang *n.m.* mud
farina *n.f.* flour
farmàcia *n.f.* pharmacy
fax *n.m.* fax
febre *n.f.* fever
febrer *n.m.* February
feliç *adj.* happy

ix = **sh**out, ll = **y**es, l·l = he**l**lo

femení *adj.* female
fer *v.* do; make
fer mal *v.* ache
ferir *v.* hurt
ferrocarril *n.m.* railway
fer-se *v.* become
fèrtil *adj.* fertile
festa *n.f.* party, festival; carnival
fet *n.m.* fact
fetge *n.m.* liver
fi *n.f.* end
figa *n.f.* fig
fil dental *n.m.* dental floss
fill *n.m.* son
filla *n.f.* daughter
finestra *n.f.* window
finir *v.* finish
fins a *prep.* until
fins que *conj.* until
fira *n.f.* fair
fixar *v.* fix
flam *n.m.* flan, custard
flama *n.f.* flame
flor *n.f.* flower
flotar *v.* float
fluir *v.* flow
fluorescent *adj.* fluorescent
FM *n.f.* FM
foca *n.f.* (*animal*) seal
fons *n.m.* bottom
for a *adv.* out
forat *n.m.* hole
forma *n.f.* shape
formatge *n.m.* cheese
formiga *n.f.* ant
forn *n.m.* oven; furnace

ç = sell, j = vision, v = boat

forn microones *n.m.* microwave oven
forquilla *n.f.* fork
fort /-a *adj.* strong
fosc /-a *adj.* dark
fotografia *n.f.* picture, photograph
fracció *n.f.* fraction
francès *n.m.* French language
francès /-esa *adj., n.* French
frankfurt *n.m.* hot dog
franqueig *n.m.* postage
fred /-a *adj.* cold
fredolic /-a *adj.* chilly
fregar *v.* rub
fregir *v.* fry, sauté
freqüent *adj.* frequent
freqüentment *adv.* frequently, often
fresc /-a *adj.* fresh; cool
front *n.m.* front; forehead
fruit *n.m.* fruit
fulla *n.f.* leaf
fum *n.m.* smoke
fumar *v.* smoke
fusta *n.f.* wood
futbol *n.m.* soccer
futbol americà *n.m.* American football

G

gabinet *n.m.* cabinet
gairebé *adv.* nearly
gal·lès /-esa *adj., n.* Welsh
galeria *n.f.* gallery
galeta *n.f.* cookie
gall dindi *n.m.* turkey
galó *n.m.* gallon
galta *n.f.* cheek

ix = **sh**out, ll = **y**es, l·l = he**ll**o

gamba *n.f.* shrimp
gana *n.f.* hunger
ganivet *n.m.* knife
gas *n.m.* gas
gasolinera *n.f.* gas station
gat *n.m.* cat
gaudir *v.* enjoy
gel *n.m.* ice
gelat *n.m.* ice cream
gelós /-osa *adj.* jealous
gelosia *n.f.* jealousy
gendre *n.m.* son-in-law
genealogia *n.f.* genealogy
gener *n.m.* January
genoll *n.m.* knee
gent *n.f.* people
gerent *n.* manager
germà *n.m.* brother
germana *n.f.* sister
gerra *n.f.* jar
ginebra *n.f.* gin
gingebre *n.m.* ginger
girar *v.* turn
gola *n.f.* throat
golf *n.m.* golf
goril·la *n.m.* gorilla
gos *n.m.* dog
got *n.m.* cup, glass
got per al vi *n.m.* wine glass
graduar *v.* graduate
gram *n.m.* gram
gramàtica *n.f.* grammar
gran *adj.* big, large; great
granger /-a *n.* farmer
granota *n.f.* frog
grau *n.m.* degree

ç = sell, j = vision, v = boat

greix *n.m.* grease
grill *n.m.* cricket
gris /-a *adj.* gray
groc /-oga *adj.* yellow
gros /-ossa *adj.* big, large, fat
grup *n.m.* group
grup sanguini *n.m.* blood type
guant *n.m.* glove
guardar *v.* keep
guerra *n.f.* war
guineu *n.f.* fox
gust *n.m.* taste

H

hamburguesa *n.f.* hamburger
hamburguesa amb formatge *n.f.*
  cheeseburger
haver (*aux.*) *v.* have
hectàrea *n.f.* hectare
hèlice *n.f.* propeller
helicòpter *n.m.* helicopter
herba *n.f.* grass
higiene *n.f.* hygiene
hivern *n.m.* winter
ho sento *interj.* sorry (I'm ~)
hola *interj.* hello
home *n.m.* man
hora *n.f.* hour
horari *n.m.* schedule
horitzó *n.m.* horizon
hospital *n.m.* hospital
hotel *n.m.* hotel
humà /-ana *adj., n.* human
humit /-ida *adj.* humid; wet
huracà *n.m.* hurricane

ix = **sh**out, ll = **y**es, l·l = he**ll**o

I

i *conj.* and
iarda *n.f.* (*measurement*) yard
idea *n.f.* idea
idioma *n.m.* language
igual *adj.* equal, same, alike
iguana *n.f.* iguana
illa *n.f.* island
imatge *n.f.* image
immediat /-a *adj.* immediate
immediatament *adv.* immediately
impermeable *n.m.* raincoat
important *adj.* important
impost *n.m.* tax
impressora *n.f.* printer
imprimir *v.* print
incendi *n.m.* fire
infecció *n.f.* infection
infeliç *adj.* unhappy
infermera *n.f.* nurse
inflar *v.* swell
iniciar *v.* begin
inquiet /-a *adj.* anxious
inscriure *v.* record
insecte *n.m.* insect, bug
inspeccionar *v.* check
instrucció *n.f.* direction
intel·ligència *n.f.* intelligence
intel·ligent *adj.* intelligent, smart
interessant *adj.* interesting
interessar *v.* care
interior *adj.* inside; inland
internet *n.m.* Internet
intèrpret *n.m.* interpreter
intestí *n.m.* intestine

inundació *n.f.* flood
invitar *v.* invite
irlandès /-esa *adj., n.* Irish
italià /-ana *adj., n.* Italian

J

ja *adv.* already
jaqueta *n.f.* jacket, coat
jardí *n.m.* garden
jeure *v.* lie down
jo *pron.* I
joc *n.m.* game
joieria *n.f.* jewelry
jove *adj.* young
joventut *n.f.* youth
jueu /-eva *adj., n.* Jew (~ish)
jugador de CD *n.m.* CD player
jugador de DVD *n.m.* DVD player
jugar *v.* play
juliol *n.m.* July
julivert *n.m.* parsley
junt *adv.* together
juntura *n.f.* joint
juny *n.m.* June
justícia *n.f.* justice

K

kosher *adj.* kosher

L

la *def. art.* the
laca *n.f.* hairspray

ix = **sh**out, ll = **yes**, l·l = hello

lamentar *v.* regret
lateralment *adv.* sideways
lavabo *n.m.* toilet
lent /-a *adj.* slow
lentament *adv.* slowly
les *pron.* them; *def. art.* the (*pl.*)
libèl·lula *n.f.* dragonfly
licor *n.m.* liquor
líder *n.* leader
línia *n.f.* line
línia aèria *n.f.* airline
líquid *n.m.* liquid
litre *n.m.* liter
llac *n.m.* lake
lladre *n.m.* thief
llagosta *n.f.* lobster; locust; grasshopper
llàgrima *n.f.* tear
llamp *n.m.* lightning
llana *n.f.* wool
llangardaix *n.m.* lizard
llapis *n.m.* pencil
llar *n.f.* home
llarg /-a *adj.* long
llavi *n.m.* lip
llavor *n.f.* seed
llavors *adv.* then
llegir *v.* read
llei *n.f.* law
lleig /-etja *adj.* ugly
llençar *v.* throw
llençol *n.m.* bedsheet, (~s) linens
llengua *n.f.* language; tongue
lleó *n.m.* lion
llesca *n.f.* slice
llescar *v.* slice
llet *n.f.* milk

ç = **sell**, j = **vision**, v = **boat**

lletra *n.f.* letter
llibre *n.m.* book
llibreria *n.f.* bookstore
llicència *n.f.* license
lliçó *n.f.* lesson
lligar *v.* attach; tie
llima *n.f.* lime
llimac *n.m.* slug
llimona *n.f.* lemon
llimonada *n.f.* lemonade
llinatge *n.m.* lineage
llit *n.m.* bed
llit de baranes *n.m.* cot
lliura *n.f.* pound
lliurar *v.* deliver; give
lliure *adj.* free
lloc de naixement *n.m.* birthplace
llogar *v.* rent
llop *n.m.* wolf
llúdria *n.f.* otter
lluitar *v.* fight
llum *n.f.* light
llum de dia *n.f.* daylight
lluna *n.f.* moon
lluny *adv.* away, far away, far off
local *adj.* local
longitud *n.f.* length

M

mà *n.f.* hand
madrastra *n.f.* stepmother
maduixa *n.f.* strawberry
màgia *n.f.* magic
mai *adv.* never
maig *n.m.* May

ix = **sh**out, ll = **y**es, l·l = he**ll**o

maionesa *n.f.* mayonnaise
majoria *n.f.* majority
mal /-a *adj.* bad
mal de cap *n.m.* headache
mal de gola *n.m.* sore throat
mal de queixal *n.m.* toothache
mal d'estómac *n.m.* stomachache
malalt /-a *adj.* sick, ill
malaltia *n.f.* disease
malgastar *v.* waste
maluc *n.m.* hip
mandíbula *n.f.* jaw
mandrós /-osa *adj.* lazy
mango *n.m.* mango
màniga *n.f.* sleeve
manta *n.f.* blanket
mantega *n.f.* butter
maó *n.m.* brick
mapa *n.m.* map
maquillar-se *v.* (*put on ~*) makeup
maquillatge *n.m.* makeup
màquina *n.f.* machine
màquina de facsímil *n.f.* fax machine
màquina de rentar *n.f.* washing machine
mar *n.* sea
maragda *n.f.* emerald
març *n.m.* March
mare *n.f.* mother, parent
marejat /-ada *adj.* dizzy; seasick
margarina *n.f.* margarine
marieta *n.f.* ladybug
marisc *n.m.* shellfish, seafood
marró *adj.* brown
marsopa *n.f.* porpoise
mascle *adj.* male
massa *n.f.* mass; *adv.* too

ç = sell, j = vision, v = boat

massatge *n.m.* massage
mastegar *v.* chew
matar *v.* kill
mateix /-a *adj.* same
matí *n.m.* morning
medicació *n.f.* medication
medicament *n.m.* medicine
mediterrani /-ània *adj., n.* Mediterranean
medusa *n.f.* jellyfish
meitat *n.f.* half
mel *n.m.* honey
meló *n.m.* cantaloupe, melon
menjador *n.m.* dining room
menjar *v.* eat
mentida *n.f.* lie
mentir *v.* lie
mentre *conj.* while
menys *adv.* less
mercat *n.m.* market
mes *n.m.* month
més *adv.* more; most; plus
més d'hora *adj.* earlier
més enllà *adv.* beyond
mescla *n.f.* mix
mesclar *v.* mix
mestre *n.m.* teacher
mesura *n.f.* measure
mesurament *n.m.* measurement
mesurar *v.* measure
metge *n.* doctor
metre *n.m.* meter
metro *n.m.* subway, metro
meu / meva *pos. adj.* my (*sing.*); *pos. pron.*
   mine (*sing.*)
meus / meves *pos. adj.* my (*pl.*); *pos. pron.*
   mine (*pl.*)

ix = **sh**out, ll = **y**es, l·l = he**ll**o

mida *n.f.* size
mig[1] *n.m.* middle
mig[2] /**-itja** *adj.* half
migdia *n.m.* noon, midday
mil *num.* thousand
mil·lilitre *n.m.* milliliter
mil·límetre *n.m.* millimeter
milla *n.f.* mile
millor *adj.* best, better
minut *n.m.* minute
mirall *n.m.* mirror
mirar *v.* look, watch, view
missatge *n.m.* message
mite *n.m.* myth
mitges *n.f.* pantyhose
mitja *adj.* average
mitjanit *n.f.* midnight
mitjó *n.m.* sock
mofeta *n.f.* skunk
molestar *v.* bother, annoy
molèstia *n.f.* trouble
moll *n.m.* wharf
molt /**-a** *adj., adv.* much; very
molts / **moltes** *adj.* many
món *n.m.* world
mona *n.f.* monkey
moneda *n.f.* money, currency; coin
moniato *n.m.* sweet potato
monitor *n.m.* monitor
morir *v.* die
morsa *n.f.* walrus
mort[1] *n.f.* death
mort[2] /**-a** *adj.* dead
mosca *n.f.* fly
mosquit *n.m.* mosquito
mossegar *v.* bite

ç = sell, j = vision, v = boat

mostassa *n.f.* mustard
mostrar *v.* show
motor *n.m.* engine
motxilla *n.f.* carry-on bag
moure *v.* move
multiplicar *v.* multiply
muntanya *n.f.* mountain
musclo *n.m.* mussel
múscul *n.m.* muscle
museu *n.m.* museum
músic *n.* musician
música *n.f.* music
musulmà /-ana *adj., n.* Muslim

N

Nadal *n.m.* Christmas
nariu *n.f.* nostril
nas *n.m.* nose
natges *n.f.* buttocks
natural *adj.* natural
navalla *n.f.* razor
navegar *v.* sail
neboda *n.f.* niece
nebot *n.m.* nephew
necessitar *v.* need
nedar *v.* swim
negoci *n.m.* business
negre /-a *adj.* black
nen /-a *n.* baby, child
neó /-ona *adj.* neon
neozelandès /-esa *n.* New Zealander
nét[1] *n.m.* grandson
nét[2] **/-a** *n.* grandchild
net /-a *adj.* clean
néta *n.f.* granddaughter

netejar *v.* clean
neu *n.f.* snow
nevar *v.* snow
nina *n.f.* doll
ningú *pron.* none
nit *n.f.* night
nit de cap d'any *n.f.* New Year's Eve
nit de Nadal *n.f.* Christmas Eve
no *adv.* no; not
no obstant *adv.* nevertheless
nodrir *v.* feed
noguera *n.f.* walnut
noi *n.m.* boy
noia *n.f.* girl
nom *n.m.* name
nora *n.f.* daughter-in-law
noranta *num.* ninety
nord *n.m.* north
nord-est *n.m.* northeast
nord-oest *n.m.* northwest
normal *adj.* normal; average
nosaltres *pron.* we
nostre / nostra *pos. adj.* our (*sing.*); *pos.
    pron.* ours (*sing.*)
nostres *pos. adj.* our (*pl.*); *pos. pron.* ours
    (*pl.*)
nota *n.f.* note
notícia *n.f.* news
nou[1] *n.f.* nut; *num.* nine
nou[2] **/-ova** *adj.* new
novembre *n.m.* November
número *n.m.* number; telephone number
nuvi *n.m.* boyfriend; groom
núvia *n.f.* girlfriend; bride
núvol *n.m.* cloud

O

o *conj.* or
obert /-a *adj.* open; on
oblidar *v.* forget
obra *n.f. (theater)* play
obrir *v.* open
obtenir *v.* get
ocasió *n.f.* occasion
occident *n.m.* west
oceà *n.m.* ocean
ocell *n.m.* bird
ocórrer *v.* occur
octubre *n.m.* October
ocupació *n.f.* job
ocupat /-ada *adj.* busy
oest *n.m.* west
ofegar *v.* choke
oficina *n.f.* office
oli *n.m.* oil
oli d'oliva *n.m.* olive oil
òliba *n.f.* owl
oliva *n.f.* olive
olla *n.f.* pot
olor *n.f.* odor, smell
olorar *v.* smell
ombra *n.f.* shadow
omplir *v.* fill
on *adv.* where
ona *n.f.* wave
oncle *n.m.* uncle
onze *num.* eleven
òpera *n.f.* opera
opinió *n.f.* opinion
oportunitat *n.f.* opportunity, chance
opòssum *n.m.* possum

ix = **sh**out, ll = **y**es, l·l = he**ll**o

or *n.m.* gold
oració *n.f.* prayer
orador *n.m.* (*person*) speaker
ordinador *n.m.* computer
orella *n.f.* ear
orient *n.m.* east
origen *n.m.* source
orina *n.f.* urine
os *n.m.* bone
ós *n.m.* bear
ós rentador *n.m.* raccoon
ostra *n.f.* oyster
ou *n.m.* egg

P

pa *n.m.* bread
padrastre *n.m.* stepfather, stepparent
padrí *n.m.* godfather, godparent
padrina *n.f.* godmother, godparent
pagament *n.m.* payment
pagar *v.* pay
pàgina *n.f.* page
país *n.m.* country
País Basc *n.m.* Basque country
paisatge *n.m.* scenery
pal *n.m.* stick
palma *n.f.* (*plant*) palm
palmell *n.m.* (*of the hand*) palm
palpar *v.* (*sensation*) feel
pantalons *n.m.* pants
pantalons curts *n.m.* shorts
papallona *n.f.* butterfly
paparra *n.f.* (*insect*) tick
paper *n.m.* paper
paper higiènic *n.m.* toilet paper

paquet *n.m.* package
paraigüa *n.m.* umbrella
parar-se *v.* stop, quit
paraula *n.f.* word
parc *n.m.* park
pare *n.m.* father, parent
parent /-a *n.* relative
paret *n.f.* wall
parir *v.* birth (give ~)
parlar *v.* speak, talk
parpella *n.f.* eyelid
part *n.f.* part
partit *n.m.* game, competition
pas *n.m.* step
Pasqua *n.f.* Easter
passaport *n.m.* passport
passat[1] *n.m.* past
passat[2] /-ada *adj.* gone
passatger /-a *n.* passenger
pasta *n.f.* pasta
pasta de dents *n.f.* toothpaste
pastanaga *n.f.* carrot
pastís *n.m.* pastry, cake
patata *n.f.* potato
pati *n.m.* (*property*) yard
pau *n.f.* peace
paviment *n.m.* floor
pebre *n.m.* (*spice*) pepper
pebrer *n.m.* pepper shaker
pebrot *n.m.* (*vegetable*) pepper
pecat *n.m.* sin
pedra *n.f.* stone
pegar *v.* hit; knock
peix *n.m.* fish
pèl *n.m.* hair
pel·lícula *n.f.* movie, film

ix = **sh**out, ll = **y**es, l·l = he**ll**o

pela *n.f.* peel
pelar *v.* peel
pell *n.f.* skin
penicil·lina *n.f.* penicillin
península *n.f.* peninsula
penis *n.m.* penis
pensament *n.m.* thought
pensar *v.* think
pentinar-se *v.* comb/brush one's hair
per *prep.* by, for; along
per cent *n.m.* percent
per què *inter. adv.* why
pera *n.f.* pear
percentatge *n.m.* percentage
perdre *v.* lose; miss
perdut /-uda *adj.* lost
perfecte /-a *adj.* perfect
perfum *n.m.* perfume
perill *n.m.* danger
perillós /-osa *adj.* dangerous
període *n.m.* period
periòdic *n.m.* newspaper
perla *n.f.* pearl
permetre *v.* permit, allow, let
pernil *n.m.* ham
però *conj.* but
perquè *conj.* because
persona *n.f.* person
personal *adj.* personal
pes *n.m.* weight
pesat /-ada *adj.* heavy
pescador *n.m.* fisherman
pescar *v.* fish
pestanya *n.f.* eyelash
pètal *n.m.* petal
petit /-a *adj.* little, small

ç = sell, j = vision, v = boat

peu *n.m.* foot
pi *n.m.* pine
piano *n.m.* piano
picar *v.* sting, bite
pijama *n.m.* pajamas
pilot *n.m.* pilot
píndola *n.f.* pill
pinta *n.f.* comb
pintallavis *n.m.* lipstick
pintura *n.f.* painting
pinya *n.f.* pineapple
piscina *n.f.* swimming pool
pista d'aterratge *n.f.* runway
pista de tenis *n.f.* tennis court
pit *n.m.* chest; breast
pizza *n.f.* pizza
planejar *v.* plan
planell *n.m.* plateau
planta *n.f.* plant
planta del peu *n.f.* sole (of the foot)
plantar *v.* plant
plat *n.m.* plate, dish
plata *n.f.* silver
plàtan *n.m.* banana
platja *n.f.* beach
ple /-ena *adj.* full
ploma *n.f.* feather; pen
plorar *v.* cry
pluja *n.f.* rain
plujós /-osa *adj.* rainy
poble *n.m.* people; village
pobre /-a *adj.* poor
pocs *adj., pron.* few
poder *n.m.* power; *v.* able (be ~)
podrit /-ida *adj.* rotten
poema *n.m.* poem

ix = **sh**out, ll = **y**es, l·l = **hello**

policia *n.f.* police
política *n.f.* politics
poll *n.m.* louse
pollastre *n.m.* chicken
pols *n.f.* dust
polzada *n.f.* inch
polze *n.m.* thumb
poma *n.f.* apple
pont *n.m.* bridge
ponx *n.m.* punch
pop *n.m.* octopus
por *n.f.* fear
porc *n.m.* pig; pork
porro *n.m.* leek
port *n.m.* port, harbor
porta *n.f.* door; gate
portar *v.* carry; bring
portàtil *n.m.* laptop computer
portuguès[1] *n.m.* Portuguese language
portuguès[2] **/-esa** *adj., n.* Portuguese
posar *v.* put
posseir *v.* own
possible *adj.* possible
posta del sol *n.f.* sunset
postres *n.f.* dessert
pot *n.m.* pot
potser *adv.* maybe, perhaps
pràctica *n.f.* practice
practicar *v.* practice
prada *n.f.* meadow
prat *n.m.* meadow
pregunta *n.f.* question
preguntar *v.* ask
prendre *v.* take
preocupar *v.* bother
preocupar-se *v.* care

ç = sell, j = vision, v = **b**oat

preocupat /-ada *adj.* worried
preparar *v.* prepare
present *adj.* present
president *n.m.* president
préssec *n.m.* peach
pressió *n.f.* pressure
pressionar *v.* squeeze
prestar *v.* lend
preu *n.m.* fare
previ /-èvia *adj.* previous
prim /-a *adj.* thin
primavera *n.f. (season)* spring
primer /-a *adj.* first
principal *adj.* main
privat /-ada *adj.* private
problema *n.m.* problem
profund /-a *adj.* deep
programari *n.m.* software
prohibit /-ida *adj.* forbidden
promesa *n.f.* promise
prometre *v.* promise
prompte *adj.* on time
pronom *n.m.* pronoun
prop de *prep.* by
proper /-a *adj.* close
propi /-òpia *adj.* proper
propietat *n.f.* ownership
protegir *v.* protect
prova *n.f.* test
provar *v.* try
proveir *v.* provide
proverbi *n.m.* proverb
pròxim /-a *adj.* next
públic /-a *adj.* public
puça *n.f.* flea
pujar *v.* climb

ix = **sh**out, ll = **y**es, l·l = he**ll**o

pulmó *n.m.* lung
puny *n.m.* fist; cuff
purpuri /-úria *adj.* purple

Q

qualitat *n.f.* quality
qualsevol *adj., pron.* any
quan *adv.* when
quantitat *n.f.* quantity
quaranta *num.* forty
quasi *adv.* almost
quatre *num.* four
que *rel. pron.* that
què *rel. pron.* what
queixar-se *v.* complain
qüestió *n.f.* question
quètxup *n.m.* ketchup
qui *pron.* who
quilogram *n.m.* kilogram
quilòmetre *n.m.* kilometer
quin /-a *inter. adj.* which, what
quinze *num.* fifteen

R

racional *adj.* rational
ràdio *n.f.* radio
raigs x *n.m.* x-ray
raïm *n.m.* grape
raó *n.f.* reason
raonable *adj.* reasonable
ràpid /-a *adj.* fast, quick
ràpidament *adv.* quickly
rar /-a *adj.* unusual, rare
rascar *v.* scratch

ç = sell, j = vision, v = boat

raspall *n.m.* brush
raspall de dents *n.m.* toothbrush
raspallar *v.* brush
rata *n.f.* rat
ratlla *n.f.* stripe
ratllar *v.* grate
ratllat /-ada *adj.* striped
ratolí *n.m.* (*animal*; *computer component*) mouse
ratpenat *n.m.* bat
reacció *n.f.* reaction
reaccionar *v.* react
real *adj.* actual
realitat *n.f.* reality
realitzar *v.* realize; achieve
realment *adv.* really, actually
rebre *v.* receive
rebut *n.m.* receipt
rebutjar *v.* dismiss (a concept)
reclinar *v.* recline
recollir *v.* collect
recompensa *n.f.* reward
reconèixer *v.* recognize
recordar *v.* remember
recordatori *n.m.* souvenir
recte /-a *adj.* straight
redactar *v.* edit
reduir *v.* reduce
reeixir *v.* succeed
refrigerador *n.m.* refrigerator
refusar *v.* refuse
regal *n.m.* gift, present
regió *n.f.* area, region
rei *n.m.* king
reina *n.f.* queen
relació *n.f.* relationship

ix = **sh**out, ll = **y**es, l·l = he**ll**o

relaxar *v.* relax
relliscar *v.* slip
rellotge *n.m.* clock; (*timepiece*) watch
rem *n.m.* oar
remar *v.* row
remoure *v.* remove
remullar *v.* soak
rentadora *n.f.* washing machine
rentar *v.* wash
rentar-se les dents *v.* brush one's teeth
repòs *n.m.* rest
reposar *v.* rest
representar *v.* represent
reproduir *v.* reproduce
requerir *v.* require
resar *v.* pray
reserva *n.f.* reservation
reservar *v.* reserve
resoldre *v.* solve
respirar *v.* breathe
respondre *v.* respond
responsable *adj.* responsible
resposta *n.f.* answer
restar *v.* subtract
restaurant *n.m.* restaurant
retornar *v.* return
reunió *n.f.* meeting
reunir-se *v.* meet
revés *n.m.* reverse
revista *n.f.* magazine
riba *n.f.* seashore, shore
ric /-a *adj.* wealthy, rich
rímmel *n.m.* mascara
riu *n.m.* river
riure *n.m.* laugh, laughter; *v.* laugh
roba *n.f.* clothing, clothes

ç = sell, j = vision, v = boat

roba interior *n.f.* underwear
robar *v.* steal, rob
robí *n.m.* ruby
roca *n.f.* rock
roda *n.f.* wheel
rodar *v.* roll
rodó /-ona *adj.* round
rom *n.m.* rum
romanç *n.m.* romance
romandre *v.* stay
romaní *n.m.* rosemary
ronyó *n.m.* kidney
ros /-sa *adj.* blond
rosat /-ada *adj.* pink
rostir *v.* broil; roast
roure *n.m.* oak
rovell *n.m.* rust
rugbi *n.m.* rugby
ruta *n.f.* route

S

sabata *n.f.* shoe
saber *n.m.* knowledge; *v.* know (something)
sabó *n.m.* soap
sabor *n.m.* flavor
sac *n.m.* bag, backpack
sacerdot *n.m.* priest
safrà *n.m.* saffron
sagnar *v.* bleed
sal *n.f.* salt
salamandra *n.f.* salamander
saler *n.m.* salt shaker
salmó *n.m.* salmon
salsa *n.f.* sauce
salsitxa *n.f.* sausage

ix = shout, ll = yes, l·l = hello

salut *n.f.* health
salvar *v.* save
salvatge *adj.* wild
samarreta *n.f.* undershirt, T-shirt
sandàlia *n.f.* sandal
sang *n.f.* blood
sardina *n.f.* sardine
satèl·lit *n.m.* satellite
satisfacció *n.f.* satisfaction
satisfer *v.* satisfy
sec /-a *adj.* dry, dried
secret[1] *n.m.* secret
secret[2] **/-a** *adj.* secret
seda *n.f.* silk
segell de correus *n.* stamp
segellar *v.* seal
segon[1] *n.m.* second
segon[2] **/-a** *adj.* second
segur[1] **/-a** *adj.* safe
segur[2] *adv.* sure
seient *n.m.* seat
seixanta *num.* sixty
selva *n.f.* jungle
semblar *v.* seem
sempre *adv.* always, forever
sentir *v.* feel (emotion); hear
senyor *n.m.* mister
senyora *n.f.* missus
separar *v.* separate, split
separat /-ada *adj.* separate
ser *v.* be (*for permanent qualities*)
serp *n.f.* snake
servir *v.* serve
set *num.* seven
setanta *num.* seventy
setembre *n.m.* September

ç = sell, j = vision, v = boat

setmana *n.f.* week

setze *num.* sixteen

seu / seva *pos. adj.* his, her, their (*sing.*); *pos. pron.* his, hers, theirs (*sing.*)

seure *v.* sit

seus / seves *pos. adj.* his, her, their (*pl.*); *pos. pron.* his, hers, theirs (*pl.*)

sexe *n.m.* sex

si *conj.* if

sí *adv.* yes

si us plau *interj.* please

SIDA *n.f.* AIDS

signatura *n.f.* signature

signe *n.m.* sign

significar *v.* mean

silenciós /-osa *adj.* quiet, silent

similar *adj.* similar, alike

simple *adj.* simple

síndria *n.f.* watermelon

sípia *n.f.* cuttlefish

sis *num.* six

sistema *n.m.* system

smoking *n.m.* tuxedo

so *n.m.* sound

sobre *adv.* over; *prep.* on; about; *n.m.* envelope

societat *n.f.* association, society

soda *n.f.* soda

sofrir *v.* suffer

sogra *n.f.* mother-in-law

sogre *n.m.* father-in-law

sol *n.m.* sun

sol /-a *adj.* alone

sola *n.f.* (*of a shoe*) sole

solament *adv.* only

somrís *n.m.* smile

ix = **sh**out, ll = **y**es, l·l = he**ll**o

somriure *v.* smile
sopa *n.f.* soup
sopar *n.m.* dinner; *v.* dine
soroll *n.m.* noise
sorollós /-osa *adj.* loud
sorpresa *n.f.* surprise
sorra *n.f.* sand
sort *n.f.* luck
sortida *n.f.* exit; departure
sortida del sol *n.f.* sunrise
sortida d'emergència *n.f.* emergency exit
sostenidor *n.m.* bra
sostre *n.m.* ceiling
sota *adv.* under, below
suar *v.* sweat
suau *adj.* smooth
súbdit *n.m.* subject
submergir *v.* dip
submergir-se *v.* dive
substància *n.f.* substance
suc *n.m.* juice, fruit juice
suc de poma *n.m.* apple juice
suc de taronja *n.m.* orange juice
sucre *n.m.* sugar
sud *n.m.* south
sud-est *n.m.* southeast
sud-oest *n.m.* southwest
suèter *n.m.* sweater
suficient *adj., adv.* enough
suggerir *v.* suggest
suite *n.f.* suite
sultar *v.* jump
suma *n.f.* amount, sum
sumar *v.* add
supermercat *n.m.* supermarket
suposar *v.* assume

ç = sell, j = vision, v = boat

suro *n.m.* cork

T

tabac *n.m.* tobacco
taca *n.f.* spot
tacat /-ada *adj.* spotted
tall *n.m.* cut
tallar *v.* cut; chop
taló *n.m.* heel
també *adv.* also, too
tan *adv.* as
tancar *v.* close, shut
tancat /-ada *adj.* closed; off
taquilla *n.f.* ticket counter
tarda *n.f.* afternoon
tardà /-ana *adj.* late
tardor *n.f.* (*season*) fall
targeta *n.f.* card
targeta de crèdit *n.f.* credit card
taronja *n.f.* orange
tasca *n.f.* job, task, assignment
tassa *n.f.* cup, glass, drinking glass
tastar *v.* taste
taula *n.f.* table, dinner table
tauró *n.m.* shark
tavallola *n.f.* towel
taverna *n.f.* pub
taxi *n.m.* taxi
te *n.m.* tea
te fred *n.m.* iced tea
teatre *n.m.* theater
teclat *n.m.* keyboard
tecnologia *n.f.* technology
teixit *n.m.* tissue
tela *n.f.* cloth

telèfon *n.m.* telephone
telèfon cel·lular *n.m.* cellular phone
telèfon mòbil *n.m.* cellular phone
televisió *n.f.* television, TV
tema *n.m.* subject
temperatura *n.f.* temperature
tempesta *n.f.* storm
tempestuós /-osa *adj.* stormy
temps *n.m.* time; weather
tenir *v.* have; hold
tenir gana *v.* be hungry
tenir por *v.* be afraid
tenir set *v.* be thirsty
terminal *n.f.* terminal
tèrmit *n.m.* termite
termòmetre *n.m.* thermometer
terra *n.f.* ground, land, earth
terra endins *adv.* inland
terratrèmol *n.m.* earthquake
tetera *n.f.* teapot
teu / teva *pos. adj.* your (*sing.*); *pos. pron.*
    yours (*sing.*)
teulada *n.f.* roof
teus / teves *pos. adj.* your (*pl.*); *pos. pron.*
    yours (*pl.*)
texans *n.m.* jeans
tia *n.f.* aunt
tigre *n.m.* tiger
tiquet *n.m.* ticket
tisores *n.f.* scissors
toc *n.m.* touch
tocar *v.* touch
tomàquet *n.m.* tomato
tona *n.f.* ton
tona mètrica *n.f.* metric ton
tonyina *n.f.* tuna

torbar *v.* embarrass
tornado *n.m.* tornado
toro *n.m.* bull
torrada *n.f.* toast
torrar *v.* toast
tortuga de mar *n.f.* turtle
tot[1] *pron.* every
tot[2] /-a *adj.* all; whole
total *n.m.* total; amount
tou /-ova *adj.* soft
tovalló *n.m.* napkin
traduir *v.* translate
tràfic *n.m.* traffic
tranquil /-il·la *adj.* still
transbordador *n.m.* ferry
transbordar *v.* transfer
transport *n.m.* transportation
travessar *v.* cross
treball *n.m.* work
treballar *v.* work
tren *n.m.* train
tren d'aterratge *n.m.* landing gear
trencar *v.* break
trenta *num.* thirty
tres *num.* three
tret que *conj.* unless
tretze *num.* thirteen
trist /-a *adj.* sad
tro *n.m.* thunder
trobar *v.* find
tròlei *n.m.* trolley
tronc *n.m.* torso
tros *n.m.* piece
tsunami *n.m.* tsunami
tu *pron.* you (*fam.*)
turista *n.* tourist

ix = **sh**out, ll = **y**es, l·l = he**ll**o

turmell *n.m.* ankle
turó *n.m.* hill
TV *n.f.* TV, television

U

ull *n.m.* eye
ulleres *n.f.* glasses, eyeglasses
últim /-a *adj.* last
un *indef. art.* a, an; *num.* one
una *indef. art.* a, an; *num.* one
una altra vegada *adv.* again
una vegada *adv.* once
unça *n.f.* ounce
unça fluida *n.f.* fluid ounce
ungla *n.f.* fingernail, toenail
universitat *n.f.* university, college
urpa *n.f.* claw
usar *v.* use
usual *adj.* usual, customary
usualment *adv.* usually

V

vaca *n.f.* cow
vacances *n.f.* vacation
vagina *n.f.* vagina
vainilla *n.f.* vanilla
vaixell *n.m.* ship, vessel, boat
vaixell de vela *n.m.* sailboat
valent /-a *adj.* bold
vall *n.f.* valley
vapor *n.m.* steam
VCR *n.m.* VCR
vegà /-ana *adj., n.* vegan
vegetarià /-ana *adj., n.* vegetarian

ç = sell, j = vision, v = boat

vehicle *n.m.* vehicle
veí *n.m.* neighbor
vela *n.f.* sail
vell /-a *adj.* old
vena *n.f.* vein
vèncer *v.* win
venda *n.f.* sale
vendre *v.* sell
venir *v.* come
vent *n.m.* wind
ventós /-osa *adj.* windy
ventre *n.m.* abdomen
verd /-a *adj.* green
verdura *n.f.* vegetable
verí *n.m.* poison
veritable *adj.* true
vermell /-a *adj.* red
vespa *n.f.* wasp
vespre *n.m.* evening
vestir *v.* dress, wear
vestit *n.m.* suit; dress
vestit de bany *n.m.* bathing suit
veu *n.f.* voice
veure *v.* see
vi *n.m.* wine
vianant *n.* pedestrian
viatge *n.m.* tour; travel
viatjar *v.* travel
vida *n.f.* life
vídeo *n.m.* video
videocasset *n.m.* video cassette
vidre *n.m.* (*substance*) glass
vidu *n.m.* widower
vídua *n.f.* widow
VIH *n.m.* HIV
vila *n.f.* town, village

ix = **sh**out, ll = **y**es, l·l = he**ll**o

vinagre *n.m.* vinegar
vint *num.* twenty
visió *n.f.* eyesight
visitar *v.* visit
vista *n.f.* view
vitamina *n.f.* vitamin
viu /-iva *adj.* alive
viure *v.* live
vodka *n.m.* vodka
vol *n.m.* flight
volar *v.* fly
volcà *n.m.* volcano
voler *v.* want
volum *n.m.* volume
vomitar *v.* vomit
vora *n.f.* edge
vosaltres *pron.* you
vostè *pron.* you (*form.*)
vostès *pron.* you
vostre / vostra *pos. adj.* your (*sing.*); *pos. pron.* yours (*sing.*)
vostres *pos. adj.* your (*pl.*); *pos. pron.* yours (*pl.*)
vot *n.m.* vote
votar *v.* vote
vuit *num.* eight
vuitanta *num.* eighty

W

whisky *n.m.* whiskey

X

xampany *n.m.* champagne
xampú *n.m.* shampoo

ç = sell, j = vision, v = boat

xarop *n.m.* syrup
xec *n.m.* (*finance*) check
xec de viatge *n.m.* traveler's check
xef *n.m.* chef
xocolata *n.f.* chocolate
xocolata desfeta *n.f.* hot chocolate
xuclar *v.* suck

Z

zero *num.* zero
zoo *n.m.* zoo

ENGLISH – CATALAN
DICTIONARY

A Note on the English Entries

Like the Catalan – English portion of this dictionary, the English – Catalan section includes part-of-speech labels that indicate the gender of nouns. However, masculine and feminine indicators ('*n.m.*' and '*n.f.*,' respectively) always refer to the Catalan word and never the English, which does not make this distinction.

See the note on page 15 about the format of the adjectives in Catalan.

ix = **sh**out, ll = **y**es, l·l = hello

A

a *indef. art.* un, una
abandon *v.* abandonar
abdomen *n.m.* abdomen, ventre
ability *n.f.* capacitat
able (be ~) *v.* poder
about *prep.* sobre
above *adv.* damunt
absent *adj.* absent
absolutely *adv.* absolutament
academy *n.f.* acadèmia
accent *n.m.* accent
accept *v.* acceptar
accessory *n.m.* accessori
accident *n.m.* accident
ache *n.m.* dolor; *v.* fer mal
achieve *v.* realitzar
acre *n.m.* acre
across *prep.* a través
act *n.m.* acte; *v.* actuar
activity *n.f.* activitat
actor *n.m.* actor
actress *n.f.* actriu
actual *adj.* real
actually *adv.* realment
A.D. *abbr.* d.C.
adapter *n.m.* adaptador
add *v.* afegir, sumar
additional *adj.* addicionao
address *n.f.* adreça
adjective *n.m.* adjectiu
adjust *v.* ajustar
admire *v.* admirar
admit *v.* admetre, confessar
adopt *v.* adoptar

ç = sell, j = vision, v = boat

adult *adj., n.* adult /-a
adverb *n.m.* adverbi
advertise *v.* anunciar
advertisement *n.m.* anunci
advice *n.m.* consell
affection *n.m.* afecte
afraid (to be ~) *v.* tenir por
after *adv.* després
afternoon *n.f.* tarda
again *adv.* una altra vegada
against *prep.* contra
age *n.f.* edat
agree *v.* acordar
ahead *adv.* davant
AIDS *n.f.* SIDA
air *n.m.* aire
air conditioner *n.m.* aire condicionat
airline *n.f.* línia aèria
airplane *n.m.* avió
airport *n.m.* aeroport
aisle *n.m.* corredor
alarm clock *n.m.* despertador
alcohol *n.m.* alcohol
algebra *n.f.* àlgebra
alike *adj.* igual
alive *adj.* viu /-iva
all *adj.* tot /-a
allergy *n.f.* al·lèrgia
alley *n.m.* carreró
alligator *n.m.* caiman
allow *v.* permetre
almond *n.f.* ametlla
almost *adv.* quasi
alone *adj.* sol /-a
along *prep.* per
alphabet *n.m.* alfabet

ix = **sh**out, ll = **y**es, l·l = he**ll**o

already *adv.* ja
also *adv.* també
always *adv.* sempre
a.m. *abbrev. See Time of Day, page 191*
ambulance *n.f.* ambulància
American *adj., n.* americà /-ana
among *prep.* entre
amount *n.m.* total; *n.f.* suma
an *indef. art.* un, una
anarchist *n.* anarquista
anarchy *n.f.* anarquia
ancestor *n.m.* avantpassat
ancient *adj.* antic /-iga
and *conj.* i
anemia *n.f.* anèmia
angel *n.m.* àngel
angle *n.m.* angle
angry *adj.* enfadat /-ada
animal *n.m.* animal
ankle *n.m.* turmell
anniversary *n.m.* aniversari
announce *v.* anunciar
annoy *v.* molestar
another *adj.* un/una altre /-a
answer *n.f.* resposta; *v.* contestar
answering machine *n.m.* contestador
   automàtic
ant *n.f.* formiga
antibiotic *n.m.* antibiòtic
antique *n.f.* antiguitat
anxious *adj.* inquiet /-a
any *adj., pron.* algun /-a; qualsevol
anybody *pron.* algú
anyone *pron.* algú
apologize *v.* disculpar-se
apology *n.f.* disculpa

appear *v.* aparèixer
appetizer *n.m.* aperitiu
applaud *v.* aplaudir
apple *n.f.* poma
apple juice *n.m.* suc de poma
appliance *n.m.* aparell
appointment *n.f.* cita
approve *v.* aprovar
April *n.m.* abril
area *n.f.* àrea, regió
arena *n.f.* arena
argue *v.* argüir
argument *n.f.* disputa
arm *n.m.* braç
around *adv.* entorn
arrest *v.* arrestar
arrival *n.f.* arribada
arrive *v.* arribar
art *n.m.* art
arthritis *n.f.* artritis
artichoke *n.f.* carxofa
artificial *adj.* artificial
artist *n.* artista
as *adv.* com; tan
ash *n.f.* cendra
ask *v.* preguntar
assignment *n.f.* tasca
association *n.f.* associació; societat
assume *v.* suposar
asthma *n.f.* asma
at *prep.* a; en
Atlantic *n.m.* Atlàntic
atlas *n.m.* atlas
ATM *n.m.* caixer automàtic
atmosphere *n.f.* atmosfera
attach *v.* lligar

ix = **sh**out, ll = **y**es, l·l = he**ll**o

attack *n.m.* atac; *v.* atacar
attend *v.* assistir
attention *n.f.* atenció
attorney *n.* advocat /-ada
attract *v.* attreure
August *n.m.* agost
aunt *n.f.* tia
Australian *adj., n.* australià /-ana
author *n.* autor
automatic *adj.* automàtic
available *adj.* disponible
avenue *n.f.* avinguda
average *adj.* mitja, normal
avoid *v.* evitar
awaken *v.* despertar
away *adv.* lluny
awkward *adj.* difícil

B

baby *n.* nen /-a
back *n.f.* esquena; *adv.* endarrera
backpack *n.m.* sac
backwards *adv.* endarrera
bacon *n.f.* cansalada
bad *adj.* mal /-a, dolent /-a
bag *n.m.* sac; *n.f.* bossa
baggage *n.m.* equipatge
bake *v.* coure
banana *n.m.* plàtan; *n.f.* banana
bandage *n.m.* embenat
bank *n.m.* banc
barbecue *n.f.* barbacoa
barge *n.f.* barcassa
bark *n.f.* escorça
baseball *n.m.* beisbol

ç = sell, j = vision, v = boat

basic *adj.* bàsic /-a
basketball *n.m.* bàsquet
Basque country *n.m.* País Basc
bat *n.m.* ratpenat
bath *n.m.* bany
bathe *v.* banyar-se
bathing suit *n.m.* vestit de bany
bathrobe *n.m.* barnús
bathroom *n.m.* bany
bathtub *n.f.* banyera
battery *n.f.* bateria
bay *n.f.* badia
B.C. *abbr.* a.C.
be *v.* ésser, ser *(for permanent qualities)*;
    estar *(for temporary qualities)*
beach *n.f.* platja
bear *n.m.* ós
beard *n.f.* barba
beat *v.* copejar
beautiful *adj.* bell /-a, bonic /-a
beauty *n.f.* bellesa
because *conj.* perquè
become *v.* esdevenir, fer-se
bed *n.m.* llit
bedroom *n.m.* dormitori
bedsheet *n.m.* llençol
bee *n.f.* abella
beef *n.f.* carn
beer *n.f.* cervesa
beetle *n.m.* escarabat
before *adv.* abans
begin *v.* començar, iniciar
behind *adv.* darrera
believe *v.* creure
bell *n.f.* campana
below *adv.* sota

ix = shout, ll = yes, l·l = hello

belt *n.m.* cinturó
berry *n.f.* baia
beside *prep.* al costat
best *adj.* millor
better *adj.* millor
between *adv.* enmig; *prep.* entre
beverage *n.f.* beguda
beyond *adv.* més enllà
bicycle *n.f.* bicicleta
big *adj.* gran, gros /-ossa
bill *n.f.* (*check*) factura
bird *n.m.* ocell
birth (give ~) *v.* parir
birthday *n.m.* aniversari
birthplace *n.m.* lloc de naixement
bite *v.* mossegar; (*to sting*) picar
black *adj.* negre /-a
blanket *n.f.* manta
bleed *v.* sagnar
blind *adj.* cec /-ega
blond *adj.* ros /-sa
blood *n.f.* sang
blood type *n.m.* grup sanguini
blouse *n.f.* brusa
blow *v.* bufar
blue *adj.* blau /-ava
blush *n.m.* (*makeup*) coloret; *v.* enrojolar-se
board *v.* embarcar
boat *n.f.* barca; *n.m.* vaixell
body *n.m.* cos
boil *v.* bullir
bold *adj.* valent /-a
bone *n.m.* os
book *n.m.* llibre
bookstore *n.f.* llibreria
boots *n.f.* botes

ç = sell, j = vision, v = **b**oat

boring *adj.* avorrit /-ida
boss *n.* cap
both *adj., pron.* ambdós /-dues
bother *v.* preocupar, molestar
bottle *n.f.* ampolla
bottom *n.m.* fons
bowl *n.m.* bol
box *n.f.* caixa, capsa
boxing *n.f.* boxa
boy *n.m.* noi
boyfriend *n.m.* nuvi
bra *n.m.* sostenidor
bracelet *n.m.* braçalet
brain *n.m.* cervell
brandy *n.m.* conyac
bread *n.m.* pa
break *v.* trencar
breakfast *n.m.* esmorzar
breast *n.m.* pit
breathe *v.* respirar
breeze *n.f.* brisa
brick *n.m.* maó
bride *n.f.* núvia
bridge *n.m.* pont
bright *adj.* brillant
bring *v.* portar
broccoli *n.m.* bròquil
broil *v.* rostir
broth *n.m.* brou
brother *n.m.* germà
brother-in-law *n.m.* cunyat
brown *adj.* marró
brush *n.m.* raspall; *v.* raspallar
brush one's hair *v.* pentinar-se
brush one's teeth *v.* rentar-se les dents
bug *n.m.* insecte

ix = **sh**out, ll = **y**es, l·l = he**ll**o

build *v.* construir
building *n.m.* edifici
bull *n.m.* toro
bullfight *n.f.* cursa de braus
burn *v.* cremar
bury *v.* enterrar
bus *n.m.* autobús
bus station *n.f.* estació de autobús
bush *n.m.* arbust
business *n.m.* negoci
busy *adj.* ocupat /-ada
but *conj.* però
butter *n.f.* mantega
butterfly *n.f.* papallona
buttocks *n.f.* natges
button *n.m.* botó
buy *v.* comprar
by *prep.* per, prop de

C

cabbage *n.f.* col
cabin *n.f.* cabina
cabinet *n.m.* gabinet
cable *n.m.* cable
cafe *n.m.* cafè
cake *n.m.* pastís
calculator *n.f.* calculadora
calendar *n.m.* calendari
call *n.f.* crida; *v.* cridar
calm *adj.* calma
camera *n.f.* càmera
Canadian *adj., n.* canadenc /-a
canary *n.m.* canari
cancel *v.* cancel·lar
candle *n.f.* espelma

ç = sell, j = vision, v = boat

candy *n.m.* dolç, caramel
canoe *n.f.* canoa
cantaloupe *n.m.* meló
canyon *n.m.* canyó
captain *n.m.* capità
car *n.m.* cotxe
car insurance *n.f.* assegurança de cotxes
card *n.f.* targeta
care *v.* interessar-se; preocupar-se
careful *adj.* acurat /-ada
cargo *n.f.* càrrega
carnival *n.f.* festa
carpet *n.f.* catifa
carrot *n.f.* pastanaga
carry *v.* portar
carry-on bag *n.f.* motxilla
castle *n.m.* castell
cat *n.m.* gat
Catalan *adj., n.* català /-ana
Catalan language *n.m.* català
catch *v.* agafar
caterpillar *n.f.* eruga
cathedral *n.f.* catedral
Catholic *adj., n.* catòlic /-a
cattle *n.m.* bestiar boví
cava *n.m.* cava
cave *n.f.* caverna
CD *n.m.* CD
CD player *n.m.* jugador de CD
ceiling *n.m.* sostre
celebrate *v.* celebrar
celebration *n.f.* celebració
celery *n.m.* api
cellular phone *n.m.* telèfon cel·lular, telèfon
  mòbil
Celsius *n.m.* Celsius

ix = **sh**out, ll = **y**es, l·l = he**ll**o

cement *n.m.* ciment
cemetery *n.m.* cementiri
center *n.m.* centre
centimeter *n.m.* centímetre
central *adj.* central
certain *adj.* cert /-a
certainly *adv.* certament
chair *n.f.* cadira
champagne *n.m.* xampany; cava
chance *n.f.* oportunitat
change *v.* canviar
charming *adj.* encantador /-a
cheap *adj.* barat /-a
check *n.m.* (*finance*) xec; *n.f.* (*bill*) factura;
    v. inspeccionar, facturar
cheek *n.f.* galta
cheese *n.m.* formatge
cheeseburger *n.f.* hamburguesa amb
    formatge
chef *n.m.* xef
cherry *n.f.* cirera
chest *n.m.* pit
chestnut *n.f.* castanya
chew *v.* mastegar
chicken *n.m.* pollastre
child *n.* nen /-a
chilly *adj.* fredolic /-a
chin *n.f.* barbeta
chocolate *n.f.* xocolata
choke *v.* ofegar
choose *v.* escollir
chop *v.* tallar
Christian *adj., n.* cristià /-ana
Christmas *n.m.* Nadal
Christmas Eve *n.f.* nit de Nadal
church *n.f.* església

ç = sell, j = vision, v = boat

cigar *n.m.* cigar
cigarette *n.m.* cigarret
cinnamon *n.f.* canyella
circle *n.m.* cercle
circus *n.m.* circ
citizen *n.m.* ciutadà
city *n.f.* ciutat
clam *n.f.* cloïssa
class *n.f.* classe
claw *n.f.* urpa
clean *adj.* net /-a; *v.* netejar
clear *adj.* clar /-a
cliff *n.m.* cingle
climb *v.* pujar
clinic *n.f.* clínica
clock *n.m.* rellotge
close *adj.* proper /-a; *v.* tancar
closed *adj.* tancat /-ada
cloth *n.f.* tela
clothes *n.f.* roba
clothing *n.f.* roba
cloud *n.m.* núvol
cloudy *adj.* ennuvolat /-ada
coast *n.f.* costa
coat *n.f.* jaqueta
cockpit *n.f.* carlinga
cockroach *n.m.* escarabat
cocktail *n.m.* còctel
coconut *n.m.* coco
cod *n.m.* bacallà
coffee *n.m.* cafè
coffee pot *n.f.* cafetera
coin *n.f.* moneda
cold *adj.* fred /-a; *n.m.* (*illness*) constipat
collar *n.m.* coll
collect *v.* recollir

ix = **sh**out, ll = **y**es, l·l = **h**ello

college *n.m.* col·legi; *n.f.* universitat
cologne *n.f.* colònia
colon *n.m.* còlon
color *n.m.* color
comb *n.f.* pinta
comb one's hair *v.* pentinar-se
combine *v.* combinar
come *v.* venir
comedy *n.f.* comèdia
comfortable *adj.* còmode /-a
comma *n.f.* coma
common *adj.* comú /-una
communicate *v.* comunicar
company *n.f.* companyia
compass *n.f.* brúixola
competition *n.m.* partit
complain *v.* queixar-se
complete *adj.* complet /-a
computer *n.m.* ordinador
concert *n.m.* concert
condiment *n.m.* condiment
congratulate *v.* congratular
connect *v.* connectar
consonant *n.f.* consonant
constant *adj.* continu /-ínua
container *n.m.* contenidor
continent *n.m.* continent
continually *adv.* continuament
continue *v.* continuar
control *v.* controlar
cook *v.* coure
cookie *n.f.* galeta
cool *adj.* fresc /-a
co-pilot *n.m.* copilot
copy *v.* copiar
cord *n.m.* cordill

ç = sell, j = vision, v = boat

cork *n.m.* suro
corn *n.m.* blat de moro
corner *n.m.* cantó
correct *adj.* correcte /-a; *v.* corregir
cost *n.m.* cost; *v.* costar
cot *n.m.* llit de baranes
count *v.* comptar
country *n.m.* país
cousin *n.* cosí /-ina
cover *n.f.* coberta; *v.* cobrir
cow *n.f.* vaca
crab *n.m.* cranc
crater *n.m.* cràter
crazy *adj.* esbojarrat -ada
cream *n.f.* crema
create *v.* crear
credit card *n.f.* targeta de crèdit
cricket *n.m.* grill
crocodile *n.m.* cocodril
cross *n.f.* creu; *v.* travessar
cry *v.* plorar; (~ **out**) cridar
cuff *n.m.* puny
culture *n.f.* cultura
cup *n.f.* tassa; *n.m.* got
cursor *n.m.* cursor
custard *n.f.* crema; *n.m.* flam
customary *adj.* usual
cut *n.m.* tall; *v.* tallar
cuttlefish *n.f.* sípia

D

dam *n.m.* dic
dance *n.m.* ball; *v.* ballar
danger *n.m.* perill
dangerous *adj.* perillós /-osa

ix = **sh**out, ll = **y**es, l·l = he**ll**o

dark *adj.* fosc /-a
date *n.f.* (*day of year*) data; (*appointment*) cita
daughter *n.f.* filla
daughter-in-law *n.f.* nora
dawn *n.f.* alba
day *n.m.* dia
daylight *n.f.* llum de dia; (*dawn*) alba
daytime *n.m.* dia
dead *adj.* mort /-a
death *n.f.* mort
debt *n.m.* deute
December *n.m.* desembre
decide *v.* decidir
deep *adj.* profund /-a
deer *n.m.* cérvol
defend *v.* defensar
define *v.* definir
definition *n.f.* definició
degree *n.m.* grau
delicate *adj.* delicat /-ada
delicious *adj.* deliciós /-osa
deliver *v.* lliurar
demonstrate *v.* demostrar
demonstration *n.f.* demostració; manifestació
dental floss *n.m.* fil dental
dentist *n.m.* dentista
deodorant *n.m.* desodorant
departure *n.f.* sortida
deposit *n.m.* dipòsit; *v.* dipositar
describe *v.* descriure
desert *n.m.* desert
desire *n.m.* desig; *v.* desitjar
dessert *n.f.* postres
destroy *v.* destruir
detail *n.m.* detall

ç = sell, j = vision, v = boat

diabetes *n.f.* diabetis
dialect *n.m.* dialecte
diamond *n.m.* diamant
dictionary *n.m.* diccionari
die *v.* morir
different *adj.* diferent
difficult *adj.* difícil
dig *v.* cavar
digital *adj.* digital
dine *v.* sopar
dining room *n.m.* menjador
dinner *n.m.* sopar
dinner table *n.f.* taula
dip *v.* submergir
direction *n.f.* direcció, instrucció
dirt *n.f.* brutícia
dirty *adj.* brut /-a
disappear *v.* desaparèixer
disappointment *n.f.* desil·lusió
disease *n.f.* malaltia
dish *n.m.* plat
dismiss *v.* (~ *a concept*) rebutjar; (~ *from somewhere*) destituir
distance *n.f.* distància
district *n.m.* districte
dive *v.* submergir-se
divide *v.* dividir
dizzy *adj.* marejat /-ada
do *v.* fer
dock *n.m.* dic
doctor *n.* metge
dog *n.m.* gos
doll *n.f.* nina
dollar *n.m.* dòlar
dolphin *n.m.* dofí
donkey *n.m.* ase

ix = **sh**out, ll = **y**es, l·l = he**ll**o

door *n.f.* porta
doubt *n.m.* dubte; *v.* dubtar
down *adv.* avall
downward *adj.* descendent
dozen *n.f.* dotzena
dragonfly *n.f.* libèl·lula
dress *n.m.* vestit; *v.* vestir
dried *adj.* sec /-a
drink *n.f.* beguda; *v.* beure
drinking glass *n.m.* got, *n.f.* tassa
drive *v.* conduir
driver *n.m.* conductor
driver's license *n.m.* carnet de conduir
drug *n.f.* droga
dry *adj.* sec /-a, àrid /-a; *v.* assecar
dryer *n.m.* (*hair* ~) eixugacabells; *n.f.*
    (*clothes* ~) assecadora
duck *n.m.* ànec
dull *adj.* avorrit /-ida
during *prep.* durant
dusk *n.m.* capvespre
dust *n.f.* pols
duty *n.m.* deure
DVD *n.m.* DVD
DVD player *n.m.* jugador de DVD

E

each *adj.* cada
ear *n.f.* orella
earlier *adj.* més d'hora
early *adj.* d'hora
earring *n.f.* arracada
earth *n.f.* terra
earthquake *n.m.* terratrèmol
east *n.m.* est, orient

ç = **s**ell, j = vi**s**ion, v = **b**oat

Easter *n.f.* Pasqua
easy *adj.* fàcil
eat *v.* menjar
economy *n.f.* economia
edge *n.f.* vora
edit *v.* redactar
eel *n.f.* anguila
effect *n.m.* efecte
effort *n.m.* esforç
egg *n.m.* ou
eggplant *n.f.* albergínia
eight *num.* vuit
eighteen *num.* divuit
eighty *num.* vuitanta
elbow *n.m.* colze
elect *v.* elegir
election *n.f.* elecció
electric *adj.* elèctric /-a
electricity *n.f.* electricitat
elevator *n.m.* ascensor
eleven *num.* onze
e-mail *n.m.* correu electrònic
embarrass *v.* torbar
embassy *n.f.* ambaixada
emerald *n.f.* maragda
emergency *n.f.* emergència
emergency exit *n.f.* sortida d'emergència
emotion *n.f.* emoció
empty *adj.* buit /-ida
end *n.f.* fi
engagement ring *n.f.* aliança
engine *n.m.* motor
English *adj., n.* anglès /-esa
English language *n.m.* anglès
enjoy *v.* gaudir
enough *adj., adv.* suficient

ix = **sh**out, ll = **y**es, l·l = he**ll**o

enter *v.* entrar
entire *adj.* enter /-a
entirely *adv.* completament
entrails *n.f.* entranyes
entrance *n.f.* entrada
envelope *n.m.* sobre
environment *n.m.* ambient
equal *adj.* igual
error *n.m.* error
evening *n.m.* vespre
event *n.m.* esdeveniment
every *pron.* tot
exact *adj.* exacte /-a
exactly *adv.* exactament
exam *n.m.* examen
example *n.m.* exemple
excellent *adj.* excel·lent
exchange *v.* canviar
excited *adj.* excitat
excursion *n.f.* excursió
exit *n.f.* sortida
expect *v.* esperar
expensive *adj.* car /-a
experience *n.f.* experiència
explain *v.* explicar
eye *n.m.* ull
eyebrow *n.f.* cella
eyeglasses *n.f.* ulleres
eyelash *n.f.* pestanya
eyelid *n.f.* parpella
eyesight *n.f.* visió

F

face *n.f.* cara
fact *n.m.* fet

ç = sell, j = vision, v = boat

Fahrenheit *n.m.* Fahrenheit
fair *n.f.* fira
fall *n.f.* caiguda; (*season*) tardor; *v.* caure
false *adj.* fals /-a
family *n.f.* família
famous *adj.* famós /-osa
far *adv.* lluny
fare *n.m.* preu
farmer *n.* granger /-a
fast *adj.* ràpid /-a
fat *adj.* gros /-ossa
father *n.m.* pare
father-in-law *n.m.* sogre
fax *n.m.* fax
fax machine *n.f.* màquina de facsímil
fear *n.f.* por
feather *n.f.* ploma
February *n.m.* febrer
feed *v.* nodrir
feel *v.* (*emotion*) sentir; (*sensation*) palpar
female *adj.* femení
ferry *n.m.* transbordador
fertile *adj.* fèrtil
festival *n.f.* festa
fever *n.f.* febre
few *adj., pron.* pocs
field *n.m.* camp
fifteen *num.* quinze
fifty *num.* cinquanta
fig *n.f.* figa
fight *v.* lluitar
fill *v.* omplir
film *n.f.* pel·lícula
find *v.* trobar
finger *n.m.* dit
fingernail *n.f.* ungla

ix = shout, ll = yes, l·l = hello

finish *v.* finir
fire *n.m.* incendi
firefly *n.f.* cuca de llum
first *adj.* primer /-a
fish *n.m.* peix; *v.* pescar
fisherman *n.m.* pescador
fist *n.m.* puny
five *num.* cinc
fix *v.* fixar
flag *n.f.* bandera
flame *n.f.* flama
flan *n.m.* flam
flavor *n.m.* sabor
flea *n.f.* puça
flesh *n.f.* carn
flight *n.m.* vol
flight attendant *n.* auxiliar de vol
float *v.* flotar
flood *n.f.* inundació
floor *n.m.* paviment
floss *n.m.* fil dental
flour *n.f.* farina
flow *v.* fluir
flower *n.f.* flor
fluorescent *adj.* fluorescent
fly *n.f.* mosca; *v.* volar
FM *n.f.* FM
fog *n.f.* boira
foggy *adj.* boirós /-osa
food *n.m.* aliment
foot *n.m.* peu
football (American) *n.m.* futbol americà
for *prep.* per
forbidden *adj.* prohibit /-ida
forehead *n.m.* front
foreign *adj.* estranger /-a

ç = sell, j = vision, v = boat

forest *n.m.* bosc
forever *adv.* sempre
forget *v.* oblidar
fork *n.f.* forquilla
forty *num.* quaranta
four *num.* quatre
fourteen *num.* catorze
fox *n.f.* guineu
fraction *n.f.* fracció
free *adj.* lliure
freeze *v.* congelar
freezer *n.m.* congelador
French *adj., n.* francès /-esa
French language *n.m.* francès
frequent *adj.* freqüent
frequently *adv.* freqüentment
fresh *adj.* fresc /-a
Friday *n.m.* divendres
friend *n.* amic /-iga
frightened *adj.* espantat /-ada
frog *n.f.* granota
from *prep.* de
front *n.m.* front; *n.f.* façana
fruit *n.m.* fruit
fruit juice *n.m.* suc
fry *v.* fregir
full *adj.* ple /-ena
fun *n.f.* broma; *v.* (**to have** ~) divertir-se
furnace *n.m.* forn

G

gallery *n.f.* galeria
gallon *n.m.* galó
game *n.m.* partit
garden *n.m.* jardí

ix = **sh**out, ll = **yes**, l·l = hello

garlic *n.m.* all
gas *n.m.* gas
gas station *n.f.* gasolinera
gate *n.f.* porta
gather *v.* acumular
genealogy *n.f.* genealogia
get *v.* obtenir
gift *n.m.* regal
gin *n.f.* ginebra
ginger *n.m.* gingebre
girl *n.f.* noia
girlfriend *n.f.* núvia
give *v.* lliurar, donar
glass *n.m.* (*substance*) vidre; *n.m.* (*cup*) got
glasses *n.f.* ulleres
glove *n.m.* guant
go *v.* anar
goat *n.f.* cabra
god *n.m.* déu
goddaughter *n.f.* afillada
godfather *n.m.* padrí
godmother *n.f.* padrina
godparent *n.* padrí /-ina
godson *n.m.* afillat
gold *n.m.* or; *adj.* d'or
golf *n.m.* golf
golf course *n.m.* camp de golf
gone *adj.* passat /-ada
good *adj.* bo /-ona
goodbye *interj., n.m.* adéu
gorilla *n.m.* goril·la
gown *n.f.* bata
grab *v.* agafar
graduate *v.* graduar
gram *n.m.* gram
grammar *n.f.* gramàtica

ç = **s**ell, j = vi**s**ion, v = **b**oat

grandchild *n.* nét /-a
granddaughter *n.f.* néta
grandfather *n.m.* avi
grandmother *n.f.* àvia
grandparents *n.m.* avis
grandson *n.m.* nét
grape *n.m.* raïm
grass *n.f.* herba
grasshopper *n.f.* llagosta
grate *v.* ratllar
gray *adj.* gris /-a
grease *n.m.* greix
great *adj.* gran
green *adj.* verd /-a
groom *n.m.* nuvi
ground *n.f.* terra
group *n.m.* grup
grow *v.* créixer

H

hail *n.f.* calamarsa; *v.* calamarsejar
hair *n.m.* pèl
hairpin *n.f.* agulla dels cabells
hairspray *n.f.* laca
half *adj.* mig /-itja; *n.f.* meitat
ham *n.m.* pernil
hamburger *n.f.* hamburguesa
hand *n.f.* mà
handsome *adj.* bell, bonic
happy *adj.* feliç
harbor *n.m.* port
hard *adj.* dur /-a
hard drive *n.m.* disc dur
hat *n.m.* barret
have *v.* tenir; (*aux.*) haver

ix = **sh**out, ll = **yes**, l·l = **hello**

hazy *adj.* bromós /-osa
he *pron.* ell
head *n.m.* cap
headache *n.m.* mal de cap
health *n.f.* salut
hear *v.* sentir
heart *n.m.* cor
heat *n.f.* calor
heater *n.m.* escalfador
heavy *adj.* pesat /-ada
hectare *n.f.* hectàrea
heel *n.m.* taló
helicopter *n.m.* helicòpter
hello *interj.* hola
help *n.m.* ajut; *v.* ajudar
her *pos. adj.* el seu, la seva, els seus, les seves; *pron. see page 11.*
here *adv.* aquí
hers *pos. pron.* el seu, la seva, els seus, les seves
hide *v.* amagar
high *adj.* alt /-a
highway *n.f.* carretera
hill *n.m.* turó
him *pron. See page 11.*
hip *n.m.* maluc
his *pos. pron., adj.* el seu, la seva, els seus, les seves
hit *v.* pegar
HIV *n.m.* VIH
hold *v.* tenir
hole *n.m.* forat
holiday *n.m.* dia de festa
home *n.f.* casa, llar
honey *n.m.* mel
horizon *n.m.* horitzó

ç = sell, j = vision, v = boat

horn *n.m.* corn
horse *n.m.* cavall
hospital *n.m.* hospital
hot *adj.* calent /-a
hot chocolate *n.f.* xocolata desfeta
hot dog *n.m.* frankfurt
hotel *n.m.* hotel
hour *n.f.* hora
house *n.f.* casa
how *adv.* com
human *adj., n.* humà /-ana
humid *adj.* humit /-ida
hundred *num.* cent
hunger *n.f.* gana
hungry (to be ~) *v.* tenir gana
hunt *v.* caçar
hurricane *n.m.* huracà
hurt *v.* ferir
husband *n.m.* espòs
hygiene *n.f.* higiene

I

I *pron.* jo
ice *n.m.* gel
ice cream *n.m.* gelat
iced tea *n.m.* te fred
idea *n.f.* idea
if *conj.* si
iguana *n.f.* iguana
ill *adj.* malalt /-a
image *n.f.* imatge
immediate *adj.* immediat /-a
immediately *adv.* immediatament
important *adj.* important
in *prep.* en

ix = **sh**out, ll = **y**es, l·l = he**ll**o

inch *n.f.* polzada
indigo *n.m.* anyil
inexpensive *adj.* barat /-a
infection *n.f.* infecció
inland *adj.* interior; *adv.* terra endins
insect *n.m.* insecte
inside *adj.* interior
intelligence *n.f.* intel·ligència
intelligent *adj.* intel·ligent
interesting *adj.* interessant
Internet *n.m.* internet
Internet café *n.m.* cibercafè
interpreter *n.m.* intèrpret
intestine *n.m.* intestí
invite *v.* invitar
Irish *adj., n.* irlandès /-esa
island *n.f.* illa
it *pron. See page 11.*
Italian *adj.* italià /-ana

J

jacket *n.f.* jaqueta
January *n.m.* gener
jar *n.f.* gerra
jaw *n.f.* mandíbula
jealous *adj.* gelós /-osa
jealousy *n.f.* gelosia
jeans *n.m.* texans
jellyfish *n.f.* medusa
Jew (~ish) *adj., n.* jueu /-eva
jewelry *n.f.* joieria
job *n.f.* ocupació, tasca
joint *n.f.* juntura
joke *n.f.* broma
juice *n.m.* suc

ç = **s**ell, j = vi**si**on, v = **b**oat

July *n.m.* juliol
jump *v.* saltar
June *n.m.* juny
jungle *n.f.* selva
justice *n.f.* justícia

K

keep *v.* guardar
ketchup *n.m.* quètxup
key *n.f.* clau
keyboard *n.m.* teclat
kidney *n.m.* ronyó
kielbasa *n.f.* salsitxa
kill *v.* matar
kilogram *n.m.* quilogram
kilometer *n.m.* quilòmetre
kind *adj.* amable
king *n.m.* rei
kiss *n.m.* bes; *v.* besar
kitchen *n.f.* cuina
knee *n.m.* genoll
knife *n.m.* ganivet
knock *v.* pegar
know *v.* (*relationships*) conèixer; (*knowledge*) saber
knowledge *n.m.* coneixement; saber
knuckle *n.m.* artell
kosher *adj.* kosher

L

ladybug *n.f.* marieta
lake *n.m.* llac
lamb *n.m.* be
land *n.f.* terra

ix = **sh**out, ll = **y**es, l·l = hel**l**o

landing *n.m.* aterratge
landing gear *n.m.* tren d'aterratge
language *n.m.* idioma, *n.f.* llengua
laptop computer *n.m.* portàtil
large *adj.* gran, gros /-ossa
last *adj.* últim /-a
last night *adv.* anit
late *adj.* tardà /-ana
later *adj.* després
laugh *n.m.* riure; *v.* riure
laughter *n.m.* riure
laundry *n.m.* rentador
law *n.f.* llei
lawyer *n.* advocat /-ada
lazy *adj.* mandrós /-osa
leaf *n.f.* fulla
leap year *n.m.* any bixest
learn *v.* aprendre
leather *n.m.* cuir
leave *v.* deixar
leek *n.m.* porro
left *adj.* esquerre /-ra
leg *n.f.* cama
lemon *n.f.* llimona
lemonade *n.f.* llimonada
lend *v.* prestar
length *n.f.* longitud
less *adv.* menys
lesson *n.f.* lliçó
let *v.* permetre
letter *n.f.* (*postal*) carta; lletra
lettuce *n.m.* enciam
license *n.f.* llicència; *n.m.* (**driver's ~**) carnet
   de conduir
lie *n.f.* mentida; *v.* mentir
lie down *v.* jeure

life *n.f.* vida
life boat *n.m.* bot salvavides
life preserver *n.m.* cinturó salvavides
light *adj.* clar /-a; *n.f.* llum
lightning *n.m.* llamp
like *adj.* similar; *adv.* com
lime *n.f.* llima
line *n.f.* línia
lineage *n.m.* llinatge
linens *n.m.* llençols
lion *n.m.* lleó
lip *n.m.* llavi
lipstick *n.m.* pintallavis
liquid *n.m.* líquid
liquor *n.m.* licor
listen *v.* escoltar
liter *n.m.* litre
little *adj.* petit /-a
live *v.* viure
liver *n.m.* fetge
lizard *n.m.* llangardaix
lobster *n.f.* llagosta
local *adj.* local
locust *n.f.* llagosta, cigala
long *adj.* llarg /-a
look *v.* mirar; (~ **for**) buscar
lose *v.* perdre
lost *adj.* perdut /-uda
loud *adj.* sorollós /-osa
louse *n.m.* poll
love *n.m.* amor; *v.* amar
lover *n.* amant
low *adj.* baix /-a
luck *n.f.* sort
lucky *adj.* afortunat /-ada
luggage *n.m.* equipatge

ix = **sh**out, ll = **y**es, l·l = **h**ello

lunch *n.m.* dinar
lung *n.m.* pulmó

M

machine *n.f.* màquina
mad *adj.* (*angry*) enfadat /-ada; (*crazy*)
   esbojarrat /-ada
magazine *n.f.* revista
magic *n.f.* màgia
maid *n.m.* criada
mail *n.m.* correu
main *adj.* principal
majority *n.f.* majoria
make *v.* (*do*) fer; (*create*) fabricar
makeup *n.m.* maquillatge; *v.* (**put on ~**)
   maquillar-se
male *adj.* mascle
mall *n.m.* centre comercial
man *n.m.* home
manager *n.m.* gerent, director
mango *n.m.* mango
many *adj.* molts, moltes (*pl.*)
map *n.m.* mapa
March *n.m.* març
margarine *n.f.* margarina
market *n.m.* mercat
marriage *n.m.* casament
married *adj.* casat /-ada
marry *v.* casar-se
mascara *n.m.* rímmel
mass *n.f.* massa
massage *n.m.* massatge
May *n.m.* maig
maybe *adv.* potser
mayonnaise *n.f.* maionesa

ç = sell, j = vision, v = boat

me *pron. see page 11.*
meadow *n.m.* prat; *n.f.* prada
meal *n.m.* àpat
mean *v.* significar
measure *n.f.* mesura; *v.* mesurar
measurement *n.m.* mesurament
meat *n.f.* carn
medication *n.f.* medicació
medicine *n.m.* medicament
Mediterranean *adj., n.* mediterrani /-ània
meet *v.* reunir-se
meeting *n.f.* reunió
melon *n.m.* meló
message *n.m.* missatge
meter *n.m.* metre
metro *n.m.* metro
metro station *n.f.* estació de metro
microwave oven *n.m.* forn microones
midday *n.m.* migdia
middle *n.m.* mig
midnight *n.f.* mitjanit
mile *n.f.* milla
milk *n.f.* llet
milliliter *n.m.* mil·lilitre
millimeter *n.m.* mil·límetre
mine *pos. pron.* el meu, la meva, els meus, les meves
minute *n.m.* minut
mirror *n.m.* mirall
mischievous *adj.* dolent /-a
miss *v.* perdre
missus (Mrs.) *n.f.* senyora
mistake *n.m.* error
mister *n.m.* senyor
mix *n.f.* mescla; *v.* mesclar
Monday *n.m.* dilluns

ix = **sh**out, ll = **y**es, l·l = he**ll**o

money *n.m.* diners, *n.f.* moneda
monitor *n.m.* monitor
monkey *n.f.* mona
month *n.m.* mes
moon *n.f.* lluna
more *adv.* més
morning *n.m.* matí
mosquito *n.m.* mosquit
most *adv.* més
moth *n.f.* arna
mother *n.f.* mare
mother-in-law *n.f.* sogra
mountain *n.f.* muntanya
mouse *n.m.* (*animal*; *computer component*) ratolí
mouth *n.f.* boca
mouthwash *n.f.* esbandida bucal
move *v.* moure
movie *n.f.* pel·lícula
movie theater *n.m.* cinema
much *adj., adv.* molt /-a
mud *n.m.* fang
multiply *v.* multiplicar
muscle *n.m.* múscul
museum *n.m.* museu
mushroom *n.m.* bolet
music *n.f.* música
musician *n.* músic
Muslim *adj., n.* musulmà /-ana
mussel *n.m.* musclo
mustard *n.f.* mostassa
my *pos. adj.* el meu, la meva, els meus, les meves
myth *n.m.* mite

ç = sell, j = vision, v = boat

N

name *n.m.* nom; *v.* anomenar
napkin *n.m.* tovalló
narrow *adj.* estret /-a
natural *adj.* natural
near *adv.* devora
nearly *adv.* gairebé
neck *n.m.* coll
necklace *n.m.* collaret
need *v.* necessitar
neighbor *n.m.* veí
neon *adj.* neó /-ona
nephew *n.m.* nebot
never *adv.* mai
nevertheless *adv.* no obstant
new *adj.* nou /-ova
New Year's Day *n.m.* any nou
New Year's Eve *n.m.* cap d'any
New Zealander *n.* neozelandès /-esa
news *n.f.* notícia
newspaper *n.m.* periòdic
next *adj.* pròxim /-a
nice *adj.* agradable
niece *n.f.* neboda
night *n.f.* nit
nine *num.* nou
nineteen *num.* dinou
ninety *num.* noranta
no *adv.* no
noise *n.m.* soroll
none *pron.* ningú
noon *n.m.* migdia
normal *adj.* normal
north *n.m.* nord
northeast *n.m.* nord-est

ix = **sh**out, ll = **yes**, l·l = **hello**

northwest *n.m.* nord-oest
nose *n.m.* nas
nostril *n.f.* nariu
not *adv.* no
note *n.f.* nota
November *n.m.* novembre
now *adv.* ara
number *n.m.* número
nurse *n.f.* infermera
nut *n.f.* nou

O

oak *n.m.* roure
oar *n.m.* rem
oat *n.f.* civada
occasion *n.f.* ocasió
occur *v.* ocórrer
ocean *n.m.* oceà
October *n.m.* octubre
octopus *n.m.* pop
odor *n.f.* olor
of *prep.* de
off *adj.* apagat /-ada
office *n.f.* oficina
often *adv.* freqüentment
oil *n.m.* oli
okay *interj.* d'acord
old *adj.* vell /-a
olive *n.f.* oliva
olive oil *n.m.* oli d'oliva
on *prep.* en, sobre; *adj.* obert /-a
on time *adj.* prompte
once *adv.* una vegada
one *num.* un, una
one-way *adj.* d'anada

ç = **s**ell, j = vi**s**ion, v = **b**oat

onion *n.f.* ceba
only *adv.* solament
open *adj.* obert /-a; *v.* obrir
opera *n.f.* òpera
opinion *n.f.* opinió
opportunity *n.f.* oportunitat
or *conj.* o
orange *n.f.* (*fruit*) taronja; *adj.* (*color*)
   ataronjat /-ada
orange juice *n.m.* suc de taronja
other *adj.* altre /-a
otter *n.f.* llúdria
ounce *n.f.* unça; (**fluid ~**) unça fluida
our *pos. adj.* el nostre, la nostra, els nostres,
   les nostres
ours *pos. pron.* el nostre, la nostra, els nostres,
   les nostres
out *adv.* fora
oven *n.m.* forn
over *adv.* sobre, damunt; *adj.* (*finished*)
   acabat /-ada
owe *v.* deure
owl *n.f.* òliba
own *v.* posseir
ownership *n.f.* propietat
oyster *n.f.* ostra

P

package *n.m.* paquet
page *n.f.* pàgina
pain *n.m.* dolor
painful *adj.* dolorós /-osa
painting *n.f.* pintura
pajamas *n.m.* pijama

palm *n.m.* (*of the hand*) palmell; *n.f.* (*plant*) palma

pan *n.m.* cassó; *n.f.* cassola

pants *n.m.* pantalons

pantyhose *n.f.* mitges

paper *n.m.* paper

parent *n.m.* pare; *n.f.* mare

parent-in-law *n.* sogre /-ra

park *n.m.* parc; *v.* aparcar

parsley *n.m.* julivert

part *n.f.* part

party *n.f.* festa

passenger *n.* passatger /-a

passport *n.m.* passaport

past *n.m.* passat

pasta *n.f.* pasta

pastry *n.m.* pastís

path *n.m.* camí

pay *v.* pagar

payment *n.m.* pagament

peace *n.f.* pau

peach *n.m.* préssec

peak *n.m.* cim

peanut *n.m.* cacauet

pear *n.f.* pera

pearl *n.f.* perla

pebble *n.m.* còdol

pedestrian *n.* vianant

peel *n.f.* pela; *v.* pelar

pen *n.m.* bolígraf

pencil *n.m.* llapis

penicillin *n.f.* penicil·lina

peninsula *n.f.* península

penis *n.m.* penis

people *n.f.* gent, *n.m.* poble

pepper *n.m.* (*spice*) pebre; (*vegetable*) pebrot

pepper shaker *n.m.* pebrer
percent *n.m.* per cent
percentage *n.m.* percentatge
perfect *adj.* perfecte /-a
perfume *n.m.* perfum
perhaps *adv.* potser
period *n.m.* període
permit *v.* permetre
person *n.f.* persona
personal *adj.* personal
petal *n.m.* pètal
pharmacy *n.f.* farmàcia
photograph *n.f.* fotografia
piano *n.m.* piano
pick *v.* (*choose*) escollir; (*pluck*) collir
picture *n.f.* fotografia
pie *n.f.* empanada
piece *n.m.* tros
pier *n.m.* dic
pig *n.m.* porc
pill *n.f.* píndola
pillow *n.m.* coixí
pilot *n.m.* pilot
pine *n.m.* pi
pineapple *n.f.* pinya
pink *adj.* rosat /-ada
pizza *n.f.* pizza
plan *v.* planejar
plant *n.f.* planta; *v.* plantar
plate *n.m.* plat
plateau *n.m.* planell
play *n.f.* (*theater*) obra; *n.m.* joc; *v.* jugar
pleasant *adj.* agradable
please *interj.* si us plau
plus *adv.* més
p.m. *abbr. See Time of Day, page 191*

ix = **sh**out, ll = **y**es, l·l = he**ll**o

pocket *n.f.* butxaca
poem *n.m.* poema
poison *n.m.* verí
police *n.f.* policia
politics *n.f.* política
pond *n.f.* bassa
poor *adj.* pobre /-a
pork *n.m.* porc
pork chop *n.f.* costella de porc
porpoise *n.f.* marsopa
port *n.m.* port
Portuguese *adj., n.* portuguès /-esa
Portuguese language *n.m.* portuguès
possible *adj.* possible
possum *n.m.* opòssum
post office *n.f.* estafeta
postage *n.m.* franqueig
pot *n.m.* pot; *n.f.* olla
potato *n.f.* patata
poultry *n.f.* aviram
pound *n.f.* lliura
power *n.m.* poder
practice *n.f.* pràctica; *v.* practicar
pray *v.* resar
prayer *n.f.* oració
pregnant *adj.* embarassada
prepare *v.* preparar
present *n.m.* regal; *adj.* present
preserve *v.* conservar
president *n.m.* president
pressure *n.f.* pressió
pretty *adj.* bonic /-a
previous *adj.* previ /-èvia
priest *n.m.* sacerdot
print *v.* imprimir
printer *n.f.* impressora

ç = **s**ell, j = vi**s**ion, v = **b**oat

private *adj.* privat /-ada
problem *n.m.* problema
promise *n.f.* promesa; *v.* prometre
pronoun *n.m.* pronom
propeller *n.f.* hèlice
proper *adj.* propi /-òpia
protect *v.* protegir
proverb *n.m.* proverbi
provide *v.* proveir
pub *n.f.* taverna
public *adj.* públic /-a
pull *v.* estirar
pumpkin *n.f.* carbassa
punch *n.m.* ponx
purple *adj.* purpuri /-úria
purse *n.f.* bossa
push *v.* empènyer
put *v.* posar
puzzle *n.m.* enigma

Q

quality *n.f.* qualitat
quantity *n.f.* quantitat
quart *n.m.* cuart
queen *n.f.* reina
question *n.f.* pregunta, qüestió
quick *adj.* ràpid /-a
quickly *adv.* ràpidament
quiet *adj.* silenciós /-osa
quit *v.* parar-se

R

rabbit *n.m.* conill
raccoon *n.m.* ós rentador

ix = **sh**out, ll = **y**es, l·l = he**l**lo

radio *n.f.* ràdio
railway *n.m.* ferrocarril
rain *n.f.* pluja
rainbow *n.m.* arc de Sant Martí
raincoat *n.m.* impermeable
rainy *adj.* plujós /-osa
raise *v.* elevar
rare *adj.* rar /-a
rat *n.f.* rata
rational *adj.* racional
raw *adj.* cru /-a
razor *n.f.* navalla
reach *v.* abastar; (*arrive*) arribar
react *v.* reaccionar
reaction *n.f.* reacció
read *v.* llegir
ready *adj.* enllestit /-ida
reality *n.f.* realitat
realize *v.* realitzar
really *adv.* realment
reason *n.f.* raó
reasonable *adj.* raonable
receipt *n.m.* rebut
receive *v.* rebre
recline *v.* reclinar
recognize *v.* reconèixer
record *v.* inscriure
red *adj.* vermell /-a
reduce *v.* reduir
refrigerator *n.m.* refrigerador
refuse *v.* refusar
regret *v.* lamentar
relationship *n.f.* relació
relative *n.* parent /-a
relax *v.* relaxar
remember *v.* recordar

ç = sell, j = vision, v = boat

remote control *n.m.* control remot
remove *v.* remoure
rent *v.* llogar
represent *v.* representar
reproduce *v.* reproduir
request *v.* demanar
require *v.* requerir
reservation *n.f.* reserva
reserve *v.* reservar
respond *v.* respondre
responsible *adj.* responsable
rest *n.m.* repòs; *v.* reposar
restaurant *n.m.* restaurant
restroom *n.m.* bany
result *n.f.* conseqüència
return *v.* retornar
reverse *n.m.* revés
reward *n.f.* recompensa
rice *n.m.* arròs
rich *adj.* ric /-a
ride *v.* cavalcar
right *adj.* dret /-a
ring *n.m.* anell; cercle
river *n.m.* riu
road *n.f.* carretera; *n.m.* camí
roast *v.* rostir
rob *v.* robar
rock *n.f.* roca
roll *v.* rodar
romance *n.m.* romanç
roof *n.f.* teulada
room *n.f.* cambra
root *n.f.* arrel
rosemary *n.m.* romaní
rotten *adj.* podrit /-ida
round *adj.* rodó /-ona

ix = **sh**out, ll = **y**es, l·l = he**ll**o

round-trip *adj.* d'anada i tornada
route *n.f.* ruta
row *v.* remar
rub *v.* fregar
ruby *n.m.* robí
rugby *n.m.* rugbi
rum *n.m.* rom
run *v.* córrer
runway *n.f.* pista d'aterratge
rust *n.m.* rovell

S

sad *adj.* trist /-a
safe *adj.* segur /-a; *n.f.* caixa forta
saffron *n.m.* safrà
sail *n.f.* vela; *v.* navegar
sailboat *n.m.* vaixell de vela
salad *n.f.* amanida
salamander *n.f.* salamandra
sale *n.f.* venda
salmon *n.m.* salmó
salt *n.f.* sal
salt shaker *n.m.* saler
same *adj.* mateix /-a, igual
sand *n.f.* sorra
sandal *n.f.* sandàlia
sandwich *n.m.* entrepà
sardine *n.f.* sardina
satellite *n.m.* satèl·lit
satisfaction *n.f.* satisfacció
satisfy *v.* satisfer
Saturday *n.m.* dissabte
sauce *n.f.* salsa
sausage *n.f.* salsitxa
sauté *v.* fregir

ç = sell, j = vision, v = boat

save *v.* salvar
say *v.* dir
saying *n.f.* dita
scar *n.f.* cicatriu
scare *v.* espantar
scenery *n.m.* paisatge
schedule *n.m.* horari
school *n.f.* escola
science *n.f.* ciència
scissors *n.f.* tisores
Scottish *adj., n.* escocès /-esa
scratch *v.* rascar
scream *n.m.* crit; *v.* cridar
sea *n.* mar
seafood *n.m.* marisc
seahorse *n.m.* cavall de mar
seal *n.f.* (*animal*) foca; *v.* segellar
search *v.* buscar
seashore *n.f.* riba, costa
seasick *adj.* marejat /-ada
season *n.f.* estació
seat *n.m.* seient
seatbelt *n.m.* cinturó de seguretat
seaward *adv.* cap al mar
seaweed *n.f.* alga
second *adj.* segon /-a; *n.m.* segon
secret *n.m.* secret; *adj.* secret /-a
see *v.* veure
seed *n.f.* llavor
seek *v.* buscar
seem *v.* semblar
sell *v.* vendre
send *v.* enviar
separate *adj.* separat /-ada; *v.* separar
September *n.m.* setembre
serve *v.* servir

ix = **sh**out, ll = yes, l·l = hello

server *n.* cambrer /-a
seven *num.* set
seventeen *num.* disset
seventy *num.* setanta
sew *v.* cosir
sex *n.m.* sexe
shadow *n.f.* ombra
shampoo *n.m.* xampú
shape *n.f.* forma
shark *n.m.* tauró
sharp *adj.* agut /-uda
shave *v.* afaitar
she *pron.* ella
sheep *n.m.* be
shell *n.f.* closca
shellfish *n.m.* marisc
shin *n.f.* canya
ship *n.m.* vaixell
shirt *n.f.* camisa
shoe *n.f.* sabata
shop *n.f.* botiga
shopping center *n.m.* centre comercial
shore *n.f.* riba, costa
short *adj.* curt /-a
shorts *n.m.* pantalons curts
shoulder *n.f.* espatlla
shout *v.* cridar
show *n.m.* espectacle; *v.* mostrar
shower *n.f.* dutxa; *v.* dutxar-se
shrimp *n.f.* gamba
shut *v.* tancar
sick *adj.* malalt /-a
side *n.m.* costat
sideways *adv.* lateralment
sign *n.m.* signe
signature *n.f.* signatura

ç = sell, j = vision, v = boat

silent *adj.* silenciós /-osa
silk *n.f.* seda
silver *n.f.* plata; *adj.* de plata
similar *adj.* similar
simple *adj.* simple
sin *n.m.* pecat
since *prep.* des de
sing *v.* cantar
sink *n.f.* aigüera; *v.* enfonsar-se
sister *n.f.* germana
sister-in-law *n.f.* cunyada
sit *v.* seure
six *num.* sis
sixteen *num.* setze
sixty *num.* seixanta
size *n.f.* mida
skin *n.f.* pell
skirt *n.f.* faldilla
skunk *n.f.* mofeta
sky *n.m.* cel
sleep *n.f.* dormida; *v.* dormir
sleet *n.f.* aiguaneu
sleeve *n.f.* màniga
slice *n.f.* llesca; *v.* llescar
slip *n.f.* (*clothing*) combinació; *v.* relliscar
slow *adj.* lent /-a
slowly *adv.* lentament
slug *n.m.* llimac
small *adj.* petit /-a
smart *adj.* intel·ligent
smell *n.f.* olor; *v.* olorar
smile *n.m.* somrís; *v.* somriure
smoke *n.m.* fum; *v.* fumar
smooth *adj.* suau
snail *n.m.* cargol
snake *n.f.* serp

ix = **sh**out, ll = **y**es, l·l = he**ll**o

sneeze *v.* esternudar
snow *n.f.* neu; *v.* nevar
soak *v.* remullar
soap *n.m.* sabó
soccer *n.m.* futbol
sock *n.m.* mitjó
soda *n.f.* soda
soft *adj.* tou /-ova
software *n.m.* programari
sole *n.f.* (*of the foot*) planta del peu; (*of a shoe*) sola
solve *v.* resoldre
some *adj.* algun /-a
sometimes *adv.* de vegades
son *n.m.* fill
song *n.f.* cançó
son-in-law *n.m.* gendre
soon *adv.* aviat
sore *adj.* dolorit /-ida
sorry (I'm ~) *interj.* ho sento
soul *n.f.* ànima
sound *n.m.* so
soup *n.f.* sopa
sour *adj.* agre /-a
source *n.m.* origen
south *n.m.* sud
southeast *n.m.* sud-est
southwest *n.m.* sud-oest
souvenir *n.m.* recordatori
Spanish *adj., n.* espanyol /-a
Spanish language *n.m.* castellà
speak *v.* parlar
speaker *n.m.* (*person*) orador
spice *n.f.* espècia
spider *n.f.* aranya
spirit *n.m.* esperit

spit *v.* escopir
split *v.* separar
spoon *n.f.* cullera
spot *n.f.* taca
spotted *adj.* tacat /-ada
spring *n.f.* (*season*) primavera
squash *n.f.* carabassa
squeeze *v.* pressionar
squid *n.m.* calamar
squirrel *n.m.* esquirol
stab *v.* apunyalar
stadium *n.m.* estadi
stamp *n.* segell de correus
stand (up) *v.* alçar-se
star *n.f.* estrella
starfish *n.f.* estrella de mar
start *v.* començar
state *n.m.* estat
station *n.f.* estació
statue *n.f.* estàtua
stay *v.* romandre
steak *n.m.* bistec
steal *v.* robar
steam *n.m.* vapor
step *n.m.* pas; *v.* caminar
stepfather *n.m.* padrastre
stepmother *n.f.* madrastra
stepparent *n.m.* padrastre; *n.f.* madrastra
stick *n.m.* pal
still *adj.* tranquil /-il·la; *adv.* encara
sting *v.* picar
stir *v.* agitar
stomach *n.m.* estómac
stomachache *n.m.* mal d'estómac
stone *n.f.* pedra
stop *v.* parar-se

ix = **sh**out, ll = **y**es, l·l = **h**ello

store *n.f.* botiga
storm *n.f.* tempesta
stormy *adj.* tempestuós /-osa
story *n.m.* conte
stove *n.f.* estufa
straight *adj.* recte /-a
strange *adj.* estrany /-a
strawberry *n.f.* maduixa
stream *n.m.* corrent
street *n.m.* carrer
stretch *v.* estirar
stripe *n.f.* ratlla
striped *adj.* ratllat /-ada
strong *adj.* fort /-a
student *n.m.* estudiant
style *n.m.* estil
subject *n.m.* súbdit; *n.m.* (*idea*) tema
substance *n.f.* substància
subtract *v.* restar
subway *n.m.* metro
subway station *n.f.* estació de metro
succeed *v.* reeixir
suck *v.* xuclar
suffer *v.* sofrir
sugar *n.m.* sucre
suggest *v.* suggerir
suit *n.m.* vestit
suite *n.f.* suite
summer *n.m.* estiu
summit *n.m.* cim
sun *n.m.* sol
Sunday *n.m.* diumenge
sunny *adj.* asolellat /-ada
sunrise *n.f.* sortida del sol
sunset *n.f.* posta del sol
supermarket *n.m.* supermercat

ç = sell, j = vision, v = boat

sure *adj.* cert /-a
surgery *n.f.* cirurgia
surname *n.m.* cognom
surprise *n.f.* sorpresa
swallow *v.* engolir
sweat *v.* suar
sweater *n.m.* suèter
sweet *adj.* dolç /-a
sweet potato *n.m.* moniato
swell *v.* inflar
swim *v.* nedar
swimming pool *n.f.* piscina
syrup *n.m.* xarop
system *n.m.* sistema

T

table *n.f.* taula
tablecloth *n.f.* estovalles
tail *n.f.* cua
take *v.* prendre, agafar
take-off *n.m.* envol
talk *v.* parlar, conversar
tall *adj.* alt /-a
task *n.f.* tasca
taste *n.m.* gust; *v.* tastar
tax *n.m.* impost
taxi *n.m.* taxi
tea *n.m.* te
teach *v.* ensenyar
teacher *n.m.* mestre
teapot *n.f.* tetera
tear *n.f.* llàgrima
technology *n.f.* tecnologia
telephone *n.m.* telèfon
telephone number *n.m.* número

ix = **sh**out, ll = **y**es, l·l = he**ll**o

television *n.f.* televisió, TV

tell *v.* dir

temperature *n.f.* temperatura

ten *num.* deu

tennis court *n.f.* pista de tenis

terminal *n.f.* terminal

termite *n.m.* tèrmit

test *n.f.* prova

thank *v.* agrair

that *dem. adj.* (*near*) aquest, aquesta, (*far*) aquell, aquella; *dem. pron.* allò; *rel. pron.* que

the *def. art.* el, els (*pl.*); la, les (*pl.*)

theater *n.m.* teatre

their *pos. adj.* el seu, la seva, els seus, les seves

theirs *pos. pron.* el seu, la seva, els seus, les seves

them *pron.* els; les

then *adv.* llavors, aleshores

there *adv.* allà, allí

thermometer *n.m.* termòmetre

these *dem. adj., pron.* aquests, aquestes

they *pron.* ells, elles

thick *adj.* espès /-essa

thief *n.m.* lladre

thigh *n.f.* cuixa

thin *adj.* prim /-a

thing *n.f.* cosa

think *v.* pensar

thirsty (to be ~) *v.* tenir set

thirteen *num.* tretze

thirty *num.* trenta

this *dem. adj.* aquest, aquesta; *dem. pron.* això

those *dem. adj., pron.* (*near*) aquests,

ç = sell, j = vision, v = boat

aquestes, (*far*) aquells, aquelles
thought *n.m.* pensament
thousand *num.* mil
three *num.* tres
throat *n.f.* gola
throw *v.* llençar
thumb *n.m.* polze
thunder *n.m.* tro
Thursday *n.m.* dijous
tick *n.f.* (*insect*) paparra
ticket *n.m.* bitllet, tiquet
ticket counter *n.f.* taquilla
tie *n.f.* corbata; *v.* lligar
tiger *n.m.* tigre
time *n.m.* temps
tired *adj.* cansat /-ada
tissue *n.m.* teixit
to *prep.* a
toast *n.f.* torrada; *v.* torrar
tobacco *n.m.* tabac
today *adv.* avui
toe *n.m.* dit del peu
toenail *n.f.* ungla del peu
together *adv.* juntament
toilet *n.m.* lavabo; bany
toilet paper *n.m.* paper higiènic
tomato *n.m.* tomàquet
tomorrow *adv.* demà
ton *n.f.* tona; (**metric ~**) tona mètrica
tongue *n.f.* llengua
tonight *adv.* aquesta nit
too *adv.* massa, (*also*) també
tooth *n.f.* dent
toothache *n.m.* mal de queixal
toothbrush *n.m.* raspall de dents
toothpaste *n.f.* pasta de dents

ix = **sh**out, ll = **y**es, l·l = he**ll**o

top *n.m.* cap
tornado *n.m.* tornado
torso *n.m.* tronc
total *n.m.* total
touch *n.m.* toc; *v.* tocar
tour *n.m.* viatge
tourist *n.* turista
toward *prep.* cap a, envers
towel *n.f.* tavallola
town *n.f.* ciutat, vila
track *n.m.* carril
traffic *n.m.* tràfic
train *n.m.* tren; *v.* entrenar
train station *n.f.* estació de tren
transfer *v.* transbordar
translate *v.* traduir
transportation *n.m.* transport
travel *n.m.* viatge; *v.* viatjar
traveler's check *n.m.* xec de viatge
tree *n.m.* arbre
trolley *n.m.* tròlei
trouble *n.f.* molèstia
truck *n.m.* camió
true *adj.* veritable, cert /-a
try *v.* provar
T-shirt *n.f.* samarreta
tsunami *n.m.* tsunami
Tuesday *n.m.* dimarts
tuna *n.f.* tonyina
turkey *n.m.* gall dindi
turn *v.* girar
turtle *n.f.* tortuga de mar
tuxedo *n.m.* smoking
TV *n.f.* TV, televisió
twelve *num.* dotze
twenty *num.* vint

ç = sell, j = vision, v = boat

twice *adv.* dos cops
two *num.* dos, dues

U

ugly *adj.* lleig /-etja
umbrella *n.m.* paraigüa
uncle *n.m.* oncle
under *adv.* sota, dessota
undershirt *n.f.* samarreta
understand *v.* entendre, comprendre
underwear *n.f.* roba interior
undo *v.* desfer
undress *v.* despullar
unhappy *adj.* infeliç
university *n.f.* universitat
unless *conj.* tret que
unpleasant *adj.* desagradable
until *conj.* fins que; *prep.* fins a
unusual *adj.* rar /-a
up *adv.* dalt
upward *adv.* cap amunt
urine *n.f.* orina
us *pron. See page 11.*
use *v.* usar
usual *adj.* usual
usually *adv.* usualment

V

vacation *n.f.* vacances
vagina *n.f.* vagina
valley *n.f.* vall
vanilla *n.f.* vainilla
VCR *n.m.* VCR
veal *n.f.* carn de vedella

ix = shout, ll = yes, l·l = hello

vegan *adj., n.* vegà /-ana
vegetable *n.f.* verdura
vegetarian *adj., n.* vegetarià /-ana
vehicle *n.m.* vehicle
vein *n.f.* vena
very *adv.* molt
vessel *n.m.* vaixell
video *n.m.* vídeo
video camera *n.f.* càmera de vídeo
video cassette *n.m.* videocasset
view *n.f.* vista; *v.* mirar
village *n.m.* poble; *n.f.* vila
vinegar *n.m.* vinagre
visit *v.* visitar
vitamin *n.f.* vitamina
vodka *n.m.* vodka
voice *n.f.* veu
voicemail *n.m.* correu de veu
volcano *n.m.* volcà
volleyball *n.m.* boleivol
volume *n.m.* volum
vomit *v.* vomitar
vote *n.m.* vot; *v.* votar

W

waist *n.f.* cintura
wait *v.* esperar
waiter *n.m.* cambrer
waitress *n.f.* cambrera
walk *v.* caminar
wall *n.f.* paret
wallet *n.f.* cartera
walnut *n.f.* noguera
walrus *n.f.* morsa
want *v.* voler

ç = sell, j = vision, v = boat

war *n.f.* guerra
warm *adj.* calent /-a
warn *v.* avisar
warning *n.m.* avís
wash *v.* rentar
washing machine *n.f.* màquina de rentar
wasp *n.f.* vespa
waste *v.* malgastar
watch *n.m.* (*timepiece*) rellotge; *v.* mirar
water *n.f.* aigua
waterfall *n.f.* cascada
watermelon *n.f.* síndria
wave *n.f.* ona
we *pron.* nosaltres
weak *adj.* dèbil
wealthy *adj.* ric /-a
wear *v.* vestir
weather *n.m.* temps
wedding *n.m.* casament
wedding ring *n.f.* aliança
Wednesday *n.m.* dimecres
week *n.f.* setmana
weekend *n.m.* cap de setmana
weight *n.m.* pes
welcome *interj.* benvingut /-uda; *v.* donar la
    benvinguda
well *adj., adv.* bé
Welsh *adj., n.* gal·lès /-esa
west *n.m.* oest, occident
wet *adj.* humit /-ida
whale *n.f.* balena
wharf *n.m.* moll
what *inter. adj.* quin /-a; *rel. pron.* què
wheat *n.m.* blat
wheel *n.f.* roda
when *adv.* quan

ix = **sh**out, ll = **y**es, l·l = he**ll**o

where *adv.* on
which *inter. adj.* quin /-a
while *conj.* mentre
whiskey *n.m.* whisky
white *adj.* blanc /-a
who *pron.* qui
whole *adj.* tot /-a
whose *pos. pron.* de qui
why *inter. adv.* per què
wide *adj.* ample /-a
widow *n.f.* vídua
widower *n.m.* vidu
wife *n.f.* esposa
wild *adj.* salvatge
win *v.* vèncer
wind *n.m.* vent
window *n.f.* finestra
windy *adj.* ventós /-osa
wine *n.m.* vi
wine glass *n.m.* got per al vi
wing *n.f.* ala
winter *n.m.* hivern
wipe *v.* eixugar
with *prep.* amb
wolf *n.m.* llop
woman *n.f.* dona
wood *n.f.* fusta
woods *n.m.* bosc
wool *n.f.* llana
word *n.f.* paraula
work *n.m.* treball; *v.* treballar
world *n.m.* món
worm *n.m.* cuc
worried *adj.* preocupat /-ada
wrist *n.m.* canell
write *v.* escriure

ç = sell, j = vision, v = boat

wrong *adj.* fals /-a

X

x-ray *n.m.* raigs x

Y

yard *n.m.* (*property*) pati; *n.f.* (*measurement*)
  iarda
year *n.m.* any
yell *v.* cridar
yellow *adj.* groc /-oga
yes *adv.* sí
yesterday *adv.* ahir
you *pron.* (*form.*) vostè, vostès; (*fam.*) tu,
  vosaltres
young *adj.* jove
your *pos. adj.* (*sing.*) el teu, la teva, els teus,
  les teves; (*pl.*) el vostre, la vostra, els
  vostres, les vostres
yours *pos. pron.* (*sing.*) el teu, la teva, els
  teus, les teves; (*pl.*) el vostre, la vostra,
  els vostres, les vostres
youth *n.f.* joventut

Z

zero *num.* zero
zipper *n.f.* cremallera
zoo *n.m.* zoo
zucchini *n.m.* carbassó

ix = **sh**out, ll = **y**es, l·l = he**ll**o

PHRASEBOOK

ESSENTIAL PHRASES

This section is comprised of some of the most practical phrases and terms in the Catalan language. Using the core structures at the beginning of this section in conjunction with the subject-specific wordlists located throughout this book the reader will be able to articulate basic thoughts, needs, and wants with minimal effort.

Core Phrases

I need …	**Necessito …**
I want (I'd like) …	**Vull …**
Can I … ?	**Puc … ?**
Can you … ?	**Pot … ?**
I have …	**Tinc …**
Do you have … ?	**Té … ?**
Is there … ?	**Hi ha … ?**
Where is … ?	**On és … ?**
What is this/that?	**Què és això?**
It/This/That is …	**És …**

How do you say … in Catalan?
Com es diu en català … ?

What does … mean?
Què vol dir … ?

Slower, please.
Més a poc a poc, si us plau.

Will you please repeat that?
Pot repetir, si us plau?

ç = sell, j = vision, v = boat

What did you say?	**Com ha dit?**
I don't understand.	**No ho entenc.**
Yes.	**Sí.**
No.	**No.**
Okay.	**D'acord.**
Please.	**Si us plau.**
Thank you.	**Gràcies.**
Thanks very much.	**Moltes gràcies.**
You're welcome.	**De res.**
I don't know.	**No ho sé.**
I'm sorry.	**Ho sento.**

Basic Questions

Who?	**Qui?**
What?	**Què?**
Where?	**On?**
When?	**Quan?**
Why?	**Per què?**
Which?	**Quin?**
How?	**Com?**

---

ix = sh**out**, ll = **yes**, l·l = he**ll**o

GREETINGS & BASIC CONVERSATION

Greetings

Hello.	**Hola.**
Welcome!	**Benvingut!** (*m.*), **Benvinguda!** (*f.*)
Good morning.	**Bon dia.**
Good afternoon.	**Bona tarda.**
Good evening.	**Bon vespre.**
Good night.	**Bona nit.**
How are you?	**Com està?** (*formal*) **Com estàs?** (*informal*)
How's it going?	**Què tal?**
I'm fine.	**Bé.**
I'm very well.	**Molt bé.**
Not very well.	**Malament.**
I'll see you later.	**Fins després.**
Goodbye.	**Adéu.**

Basic Conversational Phrases

What is your name?
Com es diu? (*formal*)
Com et dius? (*informal*)

My name is …
Em dic …

Where are you from?
D'on és vostè? *or* **D'os ets?**

ç = sell, j = vision, v = boat

I am …	**Sóc …**
American	**americà** (*m.*)
	americana (*f.*)
Australian	**australià** (*m.*)
	australiana (*f.*)
Canadian	**canadenc** (*m.*),
	canadenca (*f.*)
English	**anglès** (*m.*)
	anglesa (*f.*)
Irish	**irlandès** (*m.*)
	irlandesa (*f.*)
a New Zealander	**neozelandès** (*m.*)
	neozelandesa (*f.*)
Scottish	**escocès** (*m.*)
	escocesa (*f.*)
Welsh	**gal·lès** (*m.*)
	gal·lesa (*f.*)

Do you speak … ?	**Parla … ?**
I speak …	**Parlo …**
I don't speak …	**No parlo …**
Catalan	**català**
English	**anglès**
French	**francès**
Portuguese	**portuguès**
Spanish	**espanyol**

How old are you?
Quants anys té/tens?

I am … years old.
Tinc … anys.

See page 184 for numbers.

ix = **sh**out, ll = **y**es, l·l = he**ll**o

Nice to meet you.	**Molt de gust.** *or* **Encantat.** (*m.*) **Encantada.** (*f.*)
Nice to meet you, too.	**Igualment.**

ç = sell, j = vision, v = boat

EXCLAMATIONS & INTERJECTIONS

Absolutely!	**Absolutament!**
Amazing!	**Que sorprenent!**
Cheers!	**Salut!**
Come here!	**Vingui!**
Come on!	**Ca!**
Congratulations!	**Felicitats!**
Damn!	**Caram!**
Don't go!	**No vagi!**
Don't worry.	**No es preocupi.**
Encore!	**Un altre!**
Enjoy! *(said before dining)*	**Bon profit!**
Excellent!	**Que excel·lent!**
Excuse me. *(for attention)*	**Perdoni.**
Excuse me. *(for pardon)*	**Disculpi.**
Go away!	**Vagi!**
Good luck!	**Bona sort!**
Good!	**Que bo** (*m.*)/**bona** (*f.*)**!**
Great!	**Que fantàstic** (*m.*)/ **fantàstica** (*f.*)**!**
Hello. *(when answering a phone)*	**Digui.**
Help!	**Ajudi'm!**
Here you go. *(while offering something)*	**Tingui.**

---

ix = **sh**out, ll = **y**es, l·l = **h**ello

Hey!	**Ei!**
How beautiful!	**Que bonic** (*m.*)/ **bonica** (*f.*)!
How delicious!	**Que deliciós** (*m.*)/ **deliciosa** (*f.*)!
How strange!	**Que peculiar!**
Hurry up!	**Vingui!**
I agree!	**Estic d'acord!**
I disagree!	**No estic d'acord!**
I'm sorry.	**Ho sento.**
It doesn't matter.	**No importa.**
Let's go!	**Anem!** *or* **Som-hi!**
Let's see …	**A veure …**
Listen!	**Escolti!**
Look!	**Miri!**
Of course.	**És clar.**
Oh no!	**Ah!**
OK.	**D'acord.**
Perfect!	**Perfecte!**
Quiet!	**Calli!**
Stop!	**Pari!**
Tell me!	**Digui'm!**
Thank God/goodness!	**Gràcies a Déu!**
Uh-oh!	**Ai!**
Wait!	**Esperi'm!**
Welcome!	**Benvingut!** (*m.*) **Benvinguda!** (*f.*)
What a pity/shame!	**Quina llàstima!**

ç = sell, j = vision, v = boat

Whoa!	**Òndia!**
Whoops!	**Ai!**
Wow!	**Ui!**
Yeah!	**D'acord!**

ix = shout, ll = yes, l·l = hello

ACCOMMODATIONS

Is there a hotel nearby?
Hi ha un hotel a prop?

Where is the hotel?
On és l'hotel?

Is there a room available?
Hi ha una habitació disponible?

How much is a room for a night?
Quant costa una habitació per una nit?

I have a room reserved.
Tinc una habitació reservada.

How many nights?
Per quantes nits?

For...	Per...
one night	**una nit**
two nights	**dues nits**
one week	**una setmana**

Is there a safe?
Hi ha una caixa forta?

What time is breakfast?
A quina hora comença l'esmorzar?

What time is checkout?
A quina hora comença la sortida?

Can I have my key?
Pot donar-me la clau?

I need more toilet paper.
Necessito més paper higiènic.

The ... doesn't work.   **... no funciona.**

heat	**l'escalfador**
air conditioning	**l'aire condicionat**
hot water	**l'aigua calenta**

ç = sell, j = vision, v = boat

ACCOMMODATIONS

Related Words

air conditioner	**aire condicionat**
bathroom	**bany**
bathtub	**banyera**
bed	**llit**
bedroom	**dormitori**
bedsheets	**llençols**
blanket	**manta**
checkout	**sortida**
cot	**llit de baranes**
dining room	**menjador**
evening	**vespre**
heater	**escalfador**
hotel	**hotel**
key	**clau**
linens	**llençols**
morning	**matí**
pillow	**coixí**
pool	**piscina**
reservation	**reserva**
safe	**caixa forta**
shampoo	**xampú**
shower	**dutxa; (to ~) dutxar-se**
sleep	**dormida; (to ~) dormir**
soap	**sabó**
suite	**suite**
toilet	**lavabo**
toilet paper	**paper higiènic**
view	**vista**

ix = **sh**out, ll = **y**es, l·l = he**ll**o

TRANSPORTATION

Taxi!	**Taxi!**

How much to go to …?
Quant costa anar a …?

Take me to …	**Porti'm a …**
Where is the … ?	**On és … ?**
airport	**l'aeroport**
bus station	**l'estació de autobús**
metro/subway station	**l'estació de metro**
ticket counter/office	**la taquilla**
train station	**l'estació de tren**

How much to rent a car?
Quant costa llogar un cotxe?

I need to rent a car.
Necessito llogar un cotxe.

How much is a ticket (to …)?
Quant val un tiquet (a …)?

I need a ticket (to …).
Necessito un tiquet (a …).

I need two tickets (to …).
Necessito dos tiquets (a …).

Where is this … going?
A on va aquest … ?

Where is the … to …?
On és el … que va a …?

When will the … to … depart?
Quan marxarà el … que va a …?

ç = sell, j = vision, v = boat

When will the … to … arrive?
Quan arribarà el … que va a …?

bus	**autobús**
ferry	**transbordador**
airplane	**avió**
train	**tren**

Stop! **Pari!**

Is this the stop for …?
És aquesta la parada … ?

Related Words

airline	**línia aèria**
arrival	**arribada**
avenue	**avinguda**
baggage	**equipatge**
board	**embarcar**
check (luggage, etc.)	**facturar**
departure	**sortida**
excursion	**excursió**
fare	**preu**
flight	**vol**
gate	**porta**
luggage	**equipatge**
one-way	**d'anada**
road	**carretera**
round-trip	**d'anada i tornada**
schedule	**horari**
street	**carrer**
terminal	**terminal**
transfer	**transbordar**
turnstile	**torniquet**

ix = **sh**out, ll = **y**es, l·l = **hel**lo

DIRECTIONS

Where is the … ?

On és … ?

How do I get to … ?
Com puc arribar … ?

Can you show me on a map?
Pot indicar-m'ho a un mapa?

The … is in (the town of) ….
… és a ….

The … is on … street.
… és al carrer ….

Take … street.
Agafi el carrer ….

Go to the end of … street.
Vagi fins al final del carrer ….

Go to the end of the street.
Vagi fins al final del carrer.

Turn right.
Giri/Tombi a la dreta.

Turn left.
Giri/Tombi a l'esquerra.

The … is on the right.
… és a la dreta.

The … is on the left.
… és a l'esquerra.

Straight ahead.; Go straight.
Endavant.; Tot recte.

ç = sell, j = vision, v = boat

Compass Directions

north	**nord**
south	**sud**
east	**est**
west	**oest**
northeast	**nord-est**
northwest	**nord-oest**
southeast	**sud-est**
southwest	**sud-oest**

FOOD & DINING

Essential Phrases

I'm hungry.	**Tinc gana.**
Are you hungry?	**Té/tens gana?**
I'm thirsty.	**Tinc set.**
Are you thirsty?	**Té/tens set?**

Can you recommend a good restaurant?
Pot recomanar-me un bon restaurant?

Can you recommend a/an … restaurant?
Pot recomanar-me un restaurant … ?

inexpensive	**barat**
nice	**agradable**
local	**local**
Catalan	**català**
Italian	**italià**

May I please look at the menu?
Puc veure el menú, si us plau?

Do you have an English menu?
Té un menú en anglès?

Waiter! / Waitress!
Perdoni, cambrer (*m.*)**/cambrera** (*f.*)**!**

Do you know what you'd like to order?
Sap què vol? (*to an individual*)
Saben què volen? (*to a group*)

What do you recommend?
Què recomana?

Do you have ...?	**Tenen ...?**
What is ...?	**Què és?**
What's in this?	**Què conté?**

ç = sell, j = vision, v = boat

Is it spicy?	**És picant?**
How much is … ?	**Quant és … ?**
I'd like … / I'll have …	**Jo vull …**
Bon appetit!	**Bon profit!**

Is this what I ordered?
És què ordenava?

Check, please.
El compte, si us plau.

Other Important Phrases

Is this kosher?	**És kosher?**
I am a …	**Sóc …**
vegetarian	**vegetarià** (*m.*)
	vegetariana (*f.*)
vegan	**vegà** (*m.*), **vegana** (*f.*)

I am allergic to …
Sóc al·lèrgic (*m.*)/**al·lèrgica** (*f.*) …

nuts	**a les nous**
shellfish	**al marisc**

Beverages

I'd like … / I'll have …	**Jo vull …**
a glass/cup of …	**un got de …**
a bottle of …	**una ampolla de …**
apple juice	**suc de poma**
beer	**cervesa**
cava	**cava**
champagne	**ampany**
coffee	**cafè**

ix = **sh**out, ll = **y**es, l·l = he**ll**o

fruit juice	**suc**
gin	**ginebra**
hot chocolate	**xocolata desfeta**
ice	**gel**
iced tea	**te fred**
lemonade	**llimonada**
liquor	**licor**
milk	**llet**
orange juice	**suc de taronja**
punch	**ponx**
rum	**rom**
soda	**soda**
tea	**te**
vodka	**vodka**
water	**aigua**
(still; sparkling)	**(sense gas; amb gas)**
whiskey	**whisky**
wine (red; white)	**vi (negre; blanc)**

Menu Reader

aigua water	**blat de moro** corn
albergínia eggplant	**bolet** mushroom
alcohol alcohol	**bròquil** broccoli
all garlic	**cafè** coffee
amanida salad	**calamar** squid
arròs rice	**cansalada** bacon
aviram poultry	**canyella** cinnamon
banana banana	**carabassa** squash
be lamb	**carbassa** pumpkin
bistec steak	**carbassó** zucchini
blat wheat	**carn** beef

ç = **s**ell, j = vi**s**ion, v = **b**oat

carn de vedella veal
carxofa artichoke
cava cava
ceba onion
cervesa beer
civada oat
cloïssa clam
coco coconut
col cabbage
costella de porc pork chop
cranc crab
crema cream; custard
empanada pie
enciam lettuce
entrepà sandwich
flam flan
formatge cheese
frankfurt hot dog
galeta cookie
gall dindi turkey
gamba shrimp
gel ice
gelat ice cream
ginebra gin
gingebre ginger
hamburguesa hamburger
hamburguesa amb formatge cheeseburger
julivert parsley

licor liquor
llagosta lobster
llet milk
llima lime
llimona lemon
llimonada lemonade
maduixa strawberry
maionesa mayonnaise
mantega butter
margarina margarine
mel honey
meló cantaloupe; melon
moniato sweet potato
mostassa mustard
oli oil
oli d'oliva olive oil
oliva olive
ostra oyster
ou egg
pa bread
pasta pasta
pastanaga carrot
pastís cake
patata potato
pebre pepper (*spice*)
pebrot pepper (*vegetable*)
peix fish
pernil ham

ix = **sh**out, ll = **y**es, l·l = he**ll**o

pinya pineapple
pizza pizza
plàtan banana
pollastre chicken
poma apple
ponx punch
pop octopus
porc pork
porro leek
quètxup ketchup
raïm grape
rom rum
safrà saffron
sal salt
salsitxa sausage
síndria watermelon
soda soda

suc fruit juice
suc de poma
  apple juice
suc de taronja
  orange juice
sucre sugar
taronja orange
te tea
te fred iced tea
tomàquet tomato
vi wine
vodka vodka
whisky whiskey
xampany
  champagne
xocolata desfeta
  hot chocolate

Cooking Methods & Techniques

bake **coure**
barbecue **barbacoa**
beat **copejar**
boil **bullir**
broil **rostir**
chop **tallar**
cook **coure**
fry **fregir**

grate **ratllar**
mix **mesclar**
peel **pelar**
sauté **fregir**
slice **llesca;** (to ~)
  llescar
steam **vapor**

At the Table

bowl | **bol**
chair | **cadira**
cup | **copa**
dining room | **menjador**

ç = sell, j = vision, v = boat

dinner table	**taula**
drinking glass	**got**
fork	**forquilla**
glass	**got**
knife	**ganivet**
napkin	**tovalló**
pepper shaker	**pebrer**
plate	**plat**
salt shaker	**saler**
spoon	**cullera**
table	**taula**
tablecloth	**estovalles**
wineglass	**got per al vi**

Related Words

chef	**xef**
cocktail	**còctel**
coffee pot	**cafetera**
drink	**beguda; (to ~) beure**
eat	**menjar**
freezer	**congelador**
kitchen	**cuina**
microwave	**forn microones**
oven	**forn**
pan	**cassó, cassola**
pot	**pot, olla**
refrigerator	**refrigerador**
server	**cambrer /-a**
stove	**estufa**
teapot	**tetera**
waiter	**cambrer**
waitress	**cambrera**

ix = **sh**out, ll = yes, l·l = hello

ENTERTAINMENT

Where is the … ?
On és … ?

Can you recommend a …?
Pot recomanar-me … ?

When does the … begin?
A quina hora comença … ?

The … begins at eight o'clock.
… comença a les vuit.

(See the Time section on page 189 for further treatment of this subject.)

arena	**l'arena**
beach	**la platja**
bullfight	**la cursa de braus**
carnival	**la festa**
circus	**el circ**
competition	**el partit**
concert	**el concert**
demonstration	**la demostració**
fair	**la fira**
festival	**la festa**
game	**el partit**
golf course	**el camp de golf**
movie	**la pel·lícula**
movie theater	**el cinema**
museum	**el museu**
opera	**l'òpera**
party	**la festa**
play	**l'obra de teatre**
show	**l'espectacle**

ç = sell, j = vision, v = boat

stadium	l'estadi
swimming pool	la piscina
theater	el teatre
ticket office	la taquilla
track	el carril

How much is a ticket?
Quant val un tiquet?

I need *one ticket / two tickets*.
Necessito *un tiquet / dos tiquets*.

Related Words

baseball	beisbol
basketball	bàsquet
boxing	boxa
football	futbol americà
golf	golf
rugby	rugbi
soccer	futbol
volleyball	boleivol

PEOPLE & RELATIONSHIPS

I am …	**Sóc …**
married	**casat** (*m.*), **casada** (*f.*)
single	**solter** (*m.*), **soltera** (*f.*)
widowed	**vidu** (*m.*), **vídua** (*f.*)
divorced	**divorciat** (*m.*), **divorciada** (*f.*)

This is my husband.
Ell és el meu espòs.

This is my wife.
Ella és la meva esposa.

Are you married?
Està casat (*m.*)/**casada** (*f.*)?

Do you have children?
Té fills?

What are their names?
Els seus noms?

His/Her name is …
Ell/Ella es diu …

I have a …	**Tinc un/una …**
husband	**espòs**
wife	**esposa**
father	**par**
mother	**mare**
child	**nen** (*m.*), **nena** (*f.*)
son	**fill**
daughter	**filla**
brother	**germà**
sister	**germana**

ç = sell, j = vision, v = boat

grandfather	**avi**
grandmother	**àvia**
grandchild	**nét** (*m.*), **néta** (*f.*)
grandson	**nét**
granddaughter	**néta**
uncle	**oncle**
aunt	**tia**
nephew	**nebot**
niece	**neboda**
cousin	**cosí** (*m.*), **cosina** (*f.*)
father-in-law	**sogre**
mother-in-law	**sogra**
son-in-law	**gendre**
daughter-in-law	**nora**
brother-in-law	**cunyat**
sister-in-law	**cunyada**
stepfather	**padrastre**
stepmother	**madrastra**
godfather	**padrí**
godmother	**padrina**
godson	**afilla**
goddaughter	**afillada**

Related Words

ancestor	**avantpassat**
baby	**nen** (*m.*), **nena** (*f.*)
birth (give ~)	**parir**
boy	**noi**
family	**família**
friend	**amic** (*m.*), **amiga** (*f.*)
genealogy	**genealogia**
girl	**noia**

ix = **shout**, ll = **yes**, l·l = **hello**

grandparents	**avis**
lineage	**llinatge**
man	**home**
marriage	**casament**
marry	**casar-se**
name	**nom**
parents	**pares**
person	**persona**
relative	**parent** (*m.*), **parenta** (*f.*)
surname	**cognom**
wedding	**casament**
widow	**vídua**
widower	**vidu**
woman	**dona**

CLOTHING & ACCESSORIES

Can I try this?
Puc emprovar-me?

It's too big/small.
És massa gran/petit (*m.*), **petita** (*f.*).

I need size …
Necessito la talla …

How much?
Quant?

Clothing

bathing suit	**vestit de bany**
bathrobe	**barnús**
blouse	**brusa**
boots	**botes**
bra	**sostenidor**
coat	**jaqueta**
dress	**vestit**
glove	**guant**
gown	**bata**
hat	**barret**
jacket	**jaqueta**
jeans	**texans**
pajamas	**pijama**
pants	**pantalons**
pantyhose	**mitges**
raincoat	**impermeable**
sandals	**sandàlies**
shirt	**camisa**
shoes	**sabates**
shorts	**pantalons curts**

ix = **sh**out, ll = yes, l·l = hello

skirt	**faldilla**
slip	**combinació**
socks	**mitjons**
suit	**vestit**
sweater	**suèter**
tie	**corbata**
T-shirt	**samarreta**
tuxedo	**smoking**
undershirt	**samarreta**
underwear	**roba interior**

Accessories

belt	**cinturó**
bracelet	**braçalet**
diamond	**diamant**
earring	**arracada**
emerald	**maragda**
engagement ring	**aliança**
necklace	**collaret**
pearl	**perla**
ring	**anell**
ruby	**robí**
watch	**rellotge**
wedding ring	**aliança**

Related Words

button	**botó**
clothes	**roba**
clothing	**roba**
collar	**coll**
cuff	**puny**
dress (get ~ed)	**vestir**

ç = sell, j = vision, v = boat

jewelry	**joieria**
sleeve	**màniga**
undress	**despullar**
zipper	**cremallera**

COLORS

black	**negre /-a**
blue	**blau /-ava**
brown	**marró**
gold	**d'or**
gray	**gris /-a**
green	**verd /-a**
indigo	**anyil**
orange	**ataronjat /-ada**
pink	**rosat /-ada**
purple	**purpuri /-úria**
red	**vermell /-a**
silver	**de plata**
white	**blanc /-a**
yellow	**groc /-oga**

Related Words

artificial	**artificial**
color	**color**
dark	**fosc /-a**
fluorescent	**fluorescent**
light	**clar /-a**
natural	**natural**
neon	**neó /-ona**
spot	**taca**
spotted	**tacat /-ada**
stripe	**ratlla**
striped	**ratllat /-ada**

ç = **s**ell, j = vi**s**ion, v = **b**oat

TECHNOLOGY

Computers

computer	**ordinador**
cursor	**cursor**
digital	**digital**
e-mail	**correu electrònic**
hard drive	**disc dur**
Internet	**internet**
Internet café	**cibercafè**
keyboard	**teclat**
laptop computer	**portàtil**
monitor	**monitor**
mouse	**ratolí**
printer	**impressora**
software	**programari**

At an Internet Café

How much per (half) hour?
Quant és per una (mitja) hora?

Is there a computer available?
Hi ha un ordinador disponible?

The Internet isn't working.
L'internet no funciona.

Can I print?
Puc imprimir?

Entertainment

AM	**AM**
CD	**CD**
CD player	**jugador de CD**
DVD	**DVD**

ix = **sh**out, ll = **y**es, l·l = he**ll**o

DVD player	**jugador de DVD**
FM	**FM**
radio	**ràdio**
television	**televisió**
TV	**TV**
VCR	**VCR**
video	**vídeo**
video camera	**càmera de vídeo**
videocassette	**videocasset**

Appliances

air conditioner	**aire condicionat**
appliance	**aparell**
dryer	**assecadora**
furnace	**forn**
hair dryer	**eixugacabells**
heater	**escalfador**
microwave	**forn microones**
oven	**forn**
refrigerator	**refrigerador**
stove	**estufa**
washing machine	**rentadora**

Miscellaneous

answering machine	**contestador automàtic**
ATM	**caixer automàtic**
battery	**bateria**
cable	**cable**
calculator	**calculadora**
camera	**càmera**
cellular phone	**telèfon cel·lular;**
	telèfon mòbil

ç = sell, j = vision, v = boat

fax	**fax**
fax machine	**màquina de facsímil**
remote control	**control remot**
technology	**tecnologia**
telephone	**telèfon**
telephone number	**número**
voicemail	**correu de veu**

MEDICAL

I am ill.
Estic malalt (*m.*)/**malalta** (*f.*)**.**

I am hurt.
Estic ferit (*m.*)/**ferida** (*f.*)**.**

I need a doctor.
Necessito un metge.

Where is the … ?
On és … ?

dentist	**el dentista**
hospital	**l'hospital**
pharmacy	**la farmàcia**

It hurts here.
Em fa mal aquí.

I have …	**Tinc …**
a headache	**mal de cap**
a stomachache	**mal d'estómac**
a toothache	**mal de queixal**
anemia	**anèmia**
arthritis	**artritis**
asthma	**asma**
diabetes	**diabetis**
high blood pressure	**pressió arterial alta**
low blood pressure	**pressió arterial baixa**
HIV/AIDS	**VIH/SIDA**

I have a heart condition.
Pateixo del cor.

ç = sell, j = vision, v = boat

I am allergic to …
Sóc al·lèrgic (*m.*)/**al·lèrgica** (*f.*) …

penicillin	**a la penicil·lina**
nuts	**a les nous**
shellfish	**al marisc**

I am pregnant.
Estic embarassada.

My blood type is …
Tinc el grup sanguini …

A positive	**A positiu**
A negative	**A negatiu**
B positive	**B positiu**
B negative	**B negatiu**
AB positive	**AB positiu**
AB negative	**AB negatiu**
O positive	**O positiu**
O negative	**O negatiu**

ix = **sh**out, ll = **y**es, l·l = he**ll**o

PARTS OF THE BODY

The Body

blood	**sang**
body	**cos**
bone	**os**
brain	**cervell**
heart	**cor**
intestine	**intestí**
joint	**juntura**
kidney	**ronyó**
liver	**fetge**
lung	**pulmó**
muscle	**múscul**
skin	**pell**
stomach	**estómac**
throat	**gola**
vein	**vena**

The Head

cheek	**galta**
chin	**barbeta**
ear	**orella**
eye	**ull**
eyebrow	**cella**
eyelash	**pestanya**
eyelid	**parpella**
face	**cara**
forehead	**front**
hair	**pèl**
head	**cap**
jaw	**mandíbula**

ç = sell, j = vision, v = boat

lip	**llavi**
mouth	**boca**
neck	**coll**
nose	**nas**
nostril	**nariu**
tongue	**llengua**
tooth	**dent**

The Torso

abdomen	**abdomen, ventre**
back	**esquena**
breast	**pit**
buttocks	**natges**
chest	**pit**
hip	**maluc**
penis	**penis**
shoulder	**espatlla**
torso	**tronc**
vagina	**vagina**
waist	**cintura**

The Arm

arm	**braç**
elbow	**colze**
finger	**dit**
fingernail	**ungla**
hand	**mà**
knuckle	**artell**
palm	**palmell**
thumb	**polze**
wrist	**canell**

ix = **sh**out, ll = **y**es, l·l = he**ll**o

The Leg

ankle	**turmell**
foot	**peu**
heel	**taló**
knee	**genoll**
leg	**cama**
shin	**canya**
sole	**planta del peu**
thigh	**cuixa**
toe	**dit del peu**
toenail	**ungla del peu**

Related Words

feel	**palpar**
hear	**sentir**
look (at)	**mirar**
look (for)	**buscar**
see	**veure**
smell	**olor;** (to ~) **olorar**
taste	**gust;** (to ~) **tastar**
touch	**toc;** (to ~) **tocar**

ç = sell, j = vision, v = boat

HYGIENE

bathe	**banyar-se**
blush	**coloret**
brush one's teeth	**rentar-se les dents**
brush	**raspall**; (to ~) **raspallar**
brush/comb one's hair	**pentinar-se**
cologne	**colònia**
comb	**pinta**
dental floss	**fil dental**
deodorant	**desodorant**
hair dryer	**assecador**
hair gel	**laca**
hairpin	**agulla dels cabells**
hairspray	**laca**
hygiene	**higiene**
lipstick	**pintallavis**
makeup	**maquillatge**
mascara	**rímmel**
mirror	**mirall**
mouthwash	**esbandida bucal**
perfume	**perfum**
put on makeup	**maquillar-se**
razor	**navalla**
restroom	**bany**
shampoo	**xampú**
shave	**afaitar**
shower	**dutxa**; (to ~) **dutxar-se**
sink	**aigüera**
soap	**sabó**
tissue	**teixit**

ix = **sh**out, ll = **y**es, l·l = he**ll**o

toilet	**lavabo**
toilet paper	**paper higiènic**
toothbrush	**raspall de dents**
toothpaste	**pasta de dents**

ç = sell, j = vision, v = boat

WEATHER

I am …	**Tinc …**
hot	**calor**
cold	**fred**

What is the weather like?
Quin temps fa?

What is the weather supposed to be like?
Quin temps farà?

It is …	**Fa …**
It is supposed to be …	**Farà …**
bad weather	**mal temps**
cold	**fred**
hot	**calor**
nice	**bo**
sunny	**sol**
windy	**vent**
It is …	**Hi ha …**
It will be …	**Hi haurà …**
cloudy	**núvols**
foggy	**boira**
humid	**humitat**
It is …	**Està …**
raining	**plovent**
snowing	**nevant**
It is going to rain.	**Plourà.**
It is going to snow.	**Nevarà.**

---

ix = **sh**out, ll = yes, l·l = hello

THE ENVIRONMENT

air	**aire**
atmosphere	**atmosfera**
bay	**badia**
beach	**platja**
canyon	**canyó**
cliff	**cingle**
crater	**cràter**
dam	**dic**
desert	**desert**
environment	**ambient**
forest	**bosc**
hill	**turó**
horizon	**horitzó**
island	**illa**
jungle	**selva**
lake	**llac**
meadow	**prat, prada**
mountain	**muntanya**
ocean	**oceà**
park	**parc**
peak	**cim**
peninsula	**península**
plateau	**planell**
pond	**bassa**
river	**riu**
sea	**mar**
seashore	**cavall de mar**
sky	**cel**
stream	**corrent**
summit	**cim**

ç = sell, j = vision, v = boat

valley	**vall**
volcano	**volcà**
waterfall	**cascada**
woods	**bosc**

ANIMALS, INSECTS, & AQUATIC LIFE

Animals

bat	**ratpenat**
bear	**ós**
bird	**ocell**
bull	**toro**
cat	**gat**
cow	**vaca**
deer	**cérvol**
dog	**gos**
donkey	**ase**
fox	**guineu**
goat	**cabra**
gorilla	**goril·la**
horse	**cavall**
lamb	**be**
lion	**lleó**
monkey	**mona**
mouse	**ratolí**
pig	**porc**
possum	**opòssum**
rabbit	**conill**
raccoon	**ós rentador**
rat	**rata**
sheep	**be**
skunk	**mofeta**
squirrel	**esquirol**
tiger	**tigre**
wolf	**llop**

ç = sell, j = vision, v = boat

Insects

ant	**formiga**
bee	**abella**
beetle	**escarabat**
butterfly	**papallona**
caterpillar	**eruga**
cockroach	**escarabat**
cricket	**grill**
dragonfly	**libèl·lula**
firefly	**cuca de llum**
flea	**puça**
fly	**mosca**
grasshopper	**llagosta**
ladybug	**marieta**
locust	**llagosta, cigala**
mosquito	**mosquit**
moth	**arna**
spider	**aranya**
termite	**tèrmit**
tick	**paparra**
wasp	**vespa**
worm	**cuc**

Aquatic Life

alligator	**caiman**
clam	**cloïssa**
crab	**cranc**
crocodile	**cocodril**
dolphin	**dofí**
eel	**anguila**
fish	**peix**
frog	**granota**

ix = shout, ll = yes, l·l = hello

iguana	**iguana**
jellyfish	**medusa**
lizard	**llangardaix**
lobster	**llagosta**
mussel	**musclo**
octopus	**pop**
otter	**llúdria**
oyster	**ostra**
porpoise	**marsopa**
salamander	**salamandra**
seahorse	**cavall de mar**
seal	**foca**
shark	**tauró**
shrimp	**gamba**
slug	**llimac**
snail	**cargol**
snake	**serp**
squid	**calamar**
starfish	**estrella de mar**
turtle	**tortuga de mar**
walrus	**morsa**
whale	**balena**

ç = sell, j = vision, v = boat

EMERGENCIES

I am ill.
Estic malalt (*m.*)/**malalta** (*f.*)**.**

I am hurt.
Estic ferit (*m.*)/**ferida** (*f.*)**.**

Help!
Ajudi'm!

Stop, thief!
Lladre!

I need help!
Necessito ajuda!

I need a doctor.
Necessito un metge.

I need an ambulance.
Necessito una ambulància.

Call the police!
Truqui la policia!

I'm lost.
M'he perdut.

My … was stolen.	**Algú robava …**
I lost my …	**He perdut …**
bag	**la meva bossa**
credit card	**la meva targeta de crèdit**
medication	**la meva medicació**
money	**els meus diners**
passport	**el meu passaport**
purse	**la meva bossa**
traveler's checks	**els meus xecs de viatge**

ix = **sh**out, ll = **y**es, l·l = he**ll**o

wallet	**la meva cartera**
My … is missing.	**He perdut …**
husband	**el meu espòs**
wife	**la meva esposa**
son	**el meu fill**
daughter	**la meva filla**

ç = sell, j = vision, v = boat

NUMBERS

Because numbers act like adjectives, some numbers in Catalan reflect the gender of the noun that they describe. There are only a few of these special numbers in the cardinal set: one and two, and any number that uses these, such as thirty-one, fifty-two, two hundred, two thousand, etc. The ordinal numbers, on the other hand, always reflect gender (see *Ordinal Numbers* below for a demonstration of this).

Cardinal Numbers

0	**zero**
1	**un** (*m.*), **una** (*f.*), **u***
2	**dos** (*m.*), **dues** (*f.*)*
3	**tres**
4	**quatre**
5	**cinc**
6	**sis**
7	**set**
8	**vuit**
9	**nou**
10	**deu**
11	**onze**
12	**dotze**
13	**tretze**
14	**catorze**
15	**quinze**
16	**setze**
17	**disset**
18	**divuit**

ix = **shout**, ll = **yes**, l·l = hello

19	dinou
20	vint
21	vint-i-un / vint-i-una / vint-i-u*
22	vint-i-dos / vint-i-dues*
23	vint-i-tres
24	vint-i-quatre
25	vint-i-cinc
26	vint-i-sis
27	vint-i-set
28	vint-i-vuit
29	vint-i-nou
30	trenta
31	trenta-un / trenta-una / trenta-u*
32	trenta-dos / trenta-dues*
33	trenta-tres
34	trenta-quatre
35	trenta-cinc
36	trenta-sis
37	trenta-set
38	trenta-vuit
39	trenta-nou
40	quaranta
50	cinquanta
60	seixanta
70	setanta
80	vuitanta
90	noranta
100	cent
101	cent un / cent una / cent u*
102	cent dos / cent dues*
103	cent tres
104	cent quatre

ç = sell, j = vision, v = boat

105	cent cinc
106	cent sis
107	cent set
108	cent vuit
109	cent nou
110	cent deu
200	dos-cents / dues-centes*
300	tres-cents / tres-centes*
1000	mil
1001	mil un / mil una / mil u*
1002	mil dos / mil dues*
1003	mil tres
2000	dos mil / dues mil*
3000	tres mil
10,000	deu mil
100,000	cent mil
1,000,000	un milió

* The first of these numbers is masculine, while the second reflects the feminine gender; the third form ('u-form') is used to refer to the numbers themselves rather than the objects or ideas that they count. Example: **el numero cent u** (the number one hundred one).

Ordinal Numbers

first	primer /-a
second	segon /-a
third	tercer /-a
fourth	quart /-a
fifth	cinquè /-ena
sixth	sisè /-ena
seventh	setè /-ena

ix = shout, ll = yes, l·l = hello

eighth	**vuitè /-ena**
ninth	**novè /-ena**
tenth	**desè /-ena**
eleventh	**onzè /-ena**
twelfth	**dotzè /-ena**
thirteenth	**tretzè /-ena**
fourteenth	**catorzè /-ena**
fifteenth	**quinzè /-ena**
sixteenth	**setzè /-ena**
seventeenth	**dissetè /-ena**
eighteenth	**divuitè /-ena**
nineteenth	**dinovè /-ena**
twentieth	**vintè /-ena**
twenty-first	**vint-i-unè /-ena**
twenty-second	**vint-i-dosè /-ena**
twenty-third	**vint-i-tresè /-ena**
twenty-fourth	**vint-i-quatrè /-ena**
twenty-fifth	**vint-i-cinquè /-ena**
twenty-sixth	**vint-i-sisè /-ena**
twenty-seventh	**vint-i-setè /-ena**
twenty-eighth	**vint-i-vuitè /-ena**
twenty-ninth	**vint-i-novè /-ena**
thirtieth	**trentè /-ena**
thirty-first	**trenta-unè /-ena**

Fractions

half	**mig /-itja**
third	**terç**
quarter	**quart**
tenth	**dècim /-a**

ç = sell, j = vision, v = boat

Number Punctuation

Catalonia, like much of Europe, inverts the American number system where commas and decimal points are used. In other words, use commas where decimal points typically occur, and decimal points where you would normally use a comma. Examples: 3.619 (three thousand six hundred nineteen); 18,9 (eighteen point nine).

Related Words

add	**afegir, sumar**
amount	**total, suma**
count	**comptar**
divide	**dividir**
fraction	**fracció**
multiply	**multiplicar**
number	**número**
percent	**per cent**
percentage	**percentatge**
subtract	**restar**
total	**total**

ix = **sh**out, ll = **y**es, l·l = he**ll**o

TIME

There are several different techniques for calculating and expressing time in Catalan. Visitors to the region will find that some are decidedly more difficult to grasp than others. Speakers are always welcome to use standard time expressions, but should be aware that they will hear some rather unusual phrases, such as those employing the so-called quarter-hour system.

Basic Time Phrases

What time is it?	**Quina hora és?**
At what time?	**A quina hora?**
When?	**Quan?**

While Catalan does possess a wide variety of methods for telling time, some factors remain constant throughout the process. First, numbers are considered feminine when expressing time, and therefore take on the definite article *la* or *les*. The second factor is the distinction between singular and plural. The rule is simple, *one* is the only number to take *la*; the rest, because they are by definition more than one, take *les*. For example, *les set* (seven o'clock), *les cinc* (five o'clock), *les onze* (eleven o'clock), but *la una* (one o'clock).

Of the varied approaches to telling time in Catalan, perhaps the simplest method is to do so directly, as one might do in English:

ç = sell, j = vision, v = boat

It is ... o'clock. **Són les ...**

At ... o'clock. **A les ...**

Or, when stating the hour and the minute:

It is 9:40. **Són les nou quaranta.**

At 9:40. **A les nou quaranta.**

Speakers can also state the hour and minute with the coordinating conjunction *i* (and), as demonstrated below:

It is 9:40.
Són les nou i quaranta.

It is ten past eight o'clock.
Són les vuit i deu.

Other methods are commonly available, as well:

It is X minutes to Y o'clock.
Són les Y menys X.
(*Lit.*, It is Y minus X minutes.)

Falten X minuts per les Y.
(*Lit.*, X minutes are lacking until Y.)

Quarter-Hour System

Visitors will almost certainly hear at least some remnants of the quarter-hour system for telling time. In this system, time is counted up to the next hour in quarter-hour increments.

It is 7:15. **És un quart de vuit.**
(*Lit.*, It is one quarter of eight.)

ix = **sh**out, ll = **y**es, l·l = he**ll**o

It is 7:30.   **Són dos quarts de vuit.**
              (*Lit.*, It is two quarters of eight.)

It is 7:45.   **Són tres quarts de vuit.**
              (*Lit.*, It is three quarters of eight.)

Time of Day

Speakers of Catalan typically employ a set of terms to indicate the general time of day. These are *la matinada* (early morning), *el matí* (morning), *el migdia* (midday), *la tarda* (afternoon), *el vespre* (evening), and *la nit* (night). The use of these terms is not strictly defined, but serves simply to convey the basic sense of time of day. The terms are preceded by *de* (of); their placement in a sentence occurs after the actual time statement.

4 a.m.
les quatre de la matinada

It is 7:00 in the evening.
Són les set del vespre.

Related Words

after	**després**
before	**abans**
clock	**rellotge**
during	**durant**
earlier	**més d'hora**
early	**d'hora**
hour	**hora**
late	**tardà /-ana**
later	**després**
midnight	**mitjanit**

ç = sell, j = vision, v = boat

minute	**minut**
noon	**migdia**
now	**ara**
schedule	**horari**
second	**segon**
time	**temps**
watch	**rellotge**

---

ix = **sh**out, ll = **y**es, l·l = he**ll**o

DATES

The rules for writing and saying dates in Catalan are simple. While dates in English can take a number of different forms, Catalonians tend to favor one format in particular: dd/mm/yyyy.

Days of the Week
The days of the week are masculine nouns.

Monday	**dilluns**
Tuesday	**dimarts**
Wednesday	**dimecres**
Thursday	**dijous**
Friday	**divendres**
Saturday	**dissabte**
Sunday	**diumenge**

Months
The months are masculine nouns.

January	**gener**
February	**febrer**
March	**març**
April	**abril**
May	**maig**
June	**juny**
July	**juliol**
August	**agost**
September	**setembre**
October	**octubre**
November	**novembre**
December	**desembre**

ç = **s**ell, j = vi**s**ion, v = **b**oat

Holidays

Christmas	**Nadal**
Christmas Eve	**nit de Nadal**
Easter	**Pasqua**
New Year's Day	**any nou**
New Year's Eve	**cap d'any**

Related Words

anniversary	**aniversari**
birthday	**aniversari**
calendar	**calendari**
celebrate (to ~)	**celebrar**
celebration	**celebració**
date	**data**
day	**dia**
day after tomorrow	**demà passat**
day before yesterday	**abans d'ahir**
event	**esdeveniment**
last week	**la setmana passada**
last year	**l'any passat**
leap year	**any bixest**
meet (to ~)	**reunir-se**
meeting	**reunió**
month	**mes**
next week	**la setmana que ve**
next year	**l'any que ve**
occasion	**ocasió**
time	**temps**
today	**avui**
tomorrow	**demà**
tonight	**aquesta nit**
week	**setmana**
year	**any**
yesterday	**ahir**

ix = **sh**out, ll = yes, l·l = hello

MEASURES & CONVERSIONS

Catalonia, like all of Spain, uses the metric system of measurement. In this section the form recognized by most American users is given first, followed by the numerical equivalent of that measure in metrics. The Catalan translation for each term (with both singular and plural forms) appears beneath its English counterpart.

Size Measurements

1 inch **polzada/polzades** =
25.4 millimeters **mil·límetre(s)**
or
2.54 centimeters **centímetre(s)**

1 foot **peu(s)** = .305 meters **metre(s)**

1 yard **iarda/iardes** = .914 meters **metre(s)**

1 mile **milla/milles** = 1.61 kilometers
quilòmetre(s)

1 acre **acre(s)** = .405 hectares **hectàrea/
hectàrees**

Volume Measurements

1 fluid ounce **unça fluida/unces fluides** =
29.57 milliliters **mil·lilitre(s)**

1 quart **quart(s)** = .946 liters **litre(s)**

1 cup **tassa/tasses** = .237 liters **litre(s)**

1 gallon **galó/galons** = 3.785 liters **litre(s)**

ç = sell, j = vision, v = boat

Mass Measurements

1 ounce **unça/unces** = 28.35 grams **gram(s)**

1 pound **lliura/lliures** = .454 kilograms
quilogram(s)

1 ton **tona/tones** = .907 metric tons
**tona mètrica/
tones mètriques**

Temperature Measurements

32° Fahrenheit **grau/graus Fahrenheit** =
0° Celsius **grau/graus Celsius**

Converting Fahrenheit measurements to Celsius is as simple as performing a few mathematical operations. First, subtract thirty-two; next, multiply the new number by five; finally, divide that number by nine. The method used to convert Celsius numbers to Fahrenheit measurements is similar—multiply the Celsius number by nine, then divide the number by five, then add thirty-two.

ix = **sh**out, ll = **y**es, l·l = he**ll**o

APPENDIX:
25 CATALAN VERBS

Included here are twenty-five essential, model Catalan verbs. From these tables the reader can conjugate most other Catalan verbs; simply locate the verb in this section that possesses a similar pattern and apply the corresponding changes to the new verb. For example, if the reader wants to conjugate the verb *cantar*, simply look at the verb in the appendix whose form most resembles *cantar* (in this case the verb to be used is *caminar*, because both *cantar* and *caminar* end in -*ar* and aren't irregular).

Reading the Tables

Each of the five tenses used in this section is laid out in the following manner:

Tense Name

1st sing. 'I'	1st pl. 'we'
2nd sing. 'you' (*fam.*)	2nd pl. 'you' (*fam.*)
3rd sing. 'he/she/you' (*form.*)	3rd pl. 'they/you' (*form.*)

Caminar 'to walk' is used in the example below:

Present	camino	caminem
	camines	camineu
	camina	caminen

According to the table, then, *camino* means 'I walk,' *camines* means 'you walk,' and *cami-*

nen 'they walk,' and so on with all of the tense tables in the appendix. See the grammar section for a discussion of the meanings and uses for each tense.

anar to go

Present	vaig	anem
	vas	aneu
	va	van
Imperfect	anava	anàvem
	anaves	anàveu
	anava	anaven
Preterite	aní / vaig anar	anàrem / vam anar
	anares / vas anar	anàreu / vau anar
	anà / va anar	anaren / van anar
Future	aniré	anirem
	aniràs	anireu
	anirà	aniran
Imperative	—	anem
	vés	aneu
	vagi	vagin
Gerund	anant	

caminar to walk

Present	camino	caminem
	camines	camineu
	camina	caminen
Imperfect	caminava	caminàvem
	caminaves	caminàveu
	caminava	caminaven

Preterite	caminí / vaig caminar caminares / vas caminar caminà / va caminar	caminàrem / vam caminar caminàreu / vau caminar caminaren / van caminar
Future	caminaré caminaràs caminarà	caminarem caminareu caminaran
Imperative	— camina camini	caminem camineu caminin
Gerund	caminant	

comprar to buy

Present	compro compres compra	comprem compreu compren
Imperfect	comprava compraves comprava	compràvem compràveu compraven
Preterite	comprí / vaig comprar comprares / vas comprar comprà / va comprar	compràrem / vam comprar compràreu / vau comprar compraren / van comprar
Future	compraré compraràs comprarà	comprarem comprareu compraran
Imperative	— compra compri	comprem compreu comprin
Gerund	comprant	

conèixer to know (people, etc.)

Present	conec	coneixem
	coneixes	coneixeu
	coneix	coneixen
Imperfect	coneixia	coneixíem
	coneixies	coneixíeu
	coneixia	coneixien
Preterite	coneguí /	coneguérem /
	vaig conèixer	vam conèixer
	conegueres /	coneguéreu /
	vas conèixer	vau conèixer
	conegué /	conegueren /
	va conèixer	van conèixer
Future	coneixeré	coneixerem
	coneixeràs	coneixereu
	coneixerà	coneixeran
Imperative	—	coneguem
	coneix	coneixeu
	conegui	coneguin
Gerund	coneixent	

dir to say

Present	dic	diem
	dius	dieu
	diu	diuen
Imperfect	deia	dèiem
	deies	dèieu
	deia	deien
Preterite	diguí /	diguérem /
	vaig dir	vam dir
	digueres /	diguéreu /
	vas dir	vau dir
	digué / va dir	digueren / van dir

Future	diré	direm
	diràs	direu
	dirà	diran
Imperative	—	diguem
	digues	digueu
	digui	diguin
Gerund	dient	

entendre to understand

Present	entenc	entenem
	entens	enteneu
	entén	entenen
Imperfect	entenia	enteníem
	entenies	enteníeu
	entenia	entenien
Preterite	entenguí /	entenguérem /
	vaig entendre	vam entendre
	entengueres /	entenguéreu /
	vas entendre	vau entendre
	entengué /	entengueren /
	va entendre	van entendre
Future	entendré	entendr em
	entendràs	entendr eu
	entendrà	entendr an
Imperative	—	entenguem
	entén	enteneu
	entengui	entenguin
Gerund	entenent	

estar to be

Present	estic	estem
	estàs	esteu
	està	estan

Imperfect	estava	estàvem
	estaves	estàveu
	estava	estaven
Preterite	estiguí /	estiguérem /
	vaig estar	vam estar
	estigueres /	estiguéreu /
	vas estar	vau estar
	estigué /	estigueren /
	va estar	van estar
Future	estaré	estarem
	estaràs	estareu
	estarà	estaran
Imperative	—	estiguem
	estigues	estigueu
	estigui	estiguin
Gerund	estant	

fer to do; to make

Present	faig	fem
	fas	feu
	fa	fan
Imperfect	feia	fèiem
	feies	fèieu
	feia	feien
Preterite	fiu / vaig fer	férem / vam fer
	feres / vas fer	féreu / vau fer
	féu / va fer	feren / van fer
Future	faré	farem
	faràs	fareu
	farà	faran
Imperative	—	fem
	fes	feu
	faci	facin
Gerund	fent	

haver to have (*auxiliary verb*)

Present	he / haig	havem / hem
	has	haveu / heu
	ha	han
Imperfect	havia	havíem
	havies	havíeu
	havia	havien
Preterite	haguí /	haguérem /
	vaig haver	vam haver
	hagueres /	haguéreu /
	vas haver	vau haver
	hagué /	hagueren /
	va haver	van haver
Future	hauré	haurem
	hauràs	haureu
	haurà	hauran
Imperative	—	—
	—	—
	—	—
Gerund	havent	

parlar to speak, to talk

Present	parlo	parlem
	parles	parleu
	parla	parlen
Imperfect	parlava	parlàvem
	parlaves	parlàveu
	parlava	parlaven
Preterite	parlí /	parlàrem /
	vaig parlar	vam parlar
	parlares /	parlàreu /
	vas parlar	vau parlar
	parlà /	parlaren /
	va parlar	van parlar

Future	parlaré	parlarem
	parlaràs	parlareu
	parlarà	parlaran
Imperative	—	parlem
	parla	parleu
	parli	parlin
Gerund	parlant	

perdre to lose

Present	perdo	perdem
	perds	perdeu
	perd	perden
Imperfect	perdia	perdíem
	perdies	perdíeu
	perdia	perdien
Preterite	perdí /	perdérem /
	vaig perdre	vam perdre
	perderes /	perdéreu /
	vas perdre	vau perdre
	perdé /	perderen /
	va perdre	van perdre
Future	perdré	perdrem
	perdràs	perdreu
	perdrà	perdran
Imperative	—	perdem
	perd	perdeu
	perdi	perdin
Gerund	perdent	

poder to be able

Present	puc	podem
	pots	podeu
	pot	poden

Imperfect	podia	podíem
	podies	podíeu
	podia	podien
Preterite	poguí /	poguérem /
	vaig poder	vam poder
	pogueres /	poguéreu /
	vas poder	vau poder
	pogué /	pogueren /
	va poder	van poder
Future	podré	podrem
	podràs	podreu
	podrà	podran
Imperative	—	puguem
	pugues	pugueu
	pugui	puguin
Gerund	podent	

portar to bring, to carry

Present	porto	portem
	portes	porteu
	porta	porten
Imperfect	portava	portàvem
	portaves	portàveu
	portava	portaven
Preterite	portí /	portàrem /
	vaig portar	vam portar
	portares /	portàreu /
	vas portar	vau portar
	portà /	portaren /
	va portar	van portar
Future	portaré	portarem
	portaràs	portareu
	portarà	portaran

Imperative	—	portem
	porta	porteu
	porti	portin
Gerund	portant	

posar to put

Present	poso	posem
	poses	poseu
	posa	posen
Imperfect	posava	posàvem
	posaves	posàveu
	posava	posaven
Preterite	posí /	posàrem /
	vaig posar	vam posar
	posares /	posàreu /
	vas posar	vau posar
	posà /	posaren /
	va posar	van posar
Future	posaré	posarem
	posaràs	posareu
	posarà	posaran
Imperative	—	posem
	posa	poseu
	posi	posin
Gerund	posant	

prendre to take

Present	prenc	prenem
	prens	preneu
	pren	prenen
Imperfect	prenia	preníem
	prenies	preníeu
	prenia	prenien

Preterite	prenguí /	prenguérem /
	vaig prendre	vam prendre
	prengueres /	prenguéreu /
	vas prendre	vau prendre
	prengué /	prengueren /
	va prendre	van prendre
Future	prendré	prendrem
	prendràs	prendreu
	prendrà	prendran
Imperative	—	prenguem
	pren	preneu
	prengui	prenguin
Gerund	prenent	

saber to know (information, etc.)

Present	sé	sabem
Imperfect	saps	sabeu
	sap	saben
Imperfect	sabia	sabíem
	sabies	sabíeu
	sabia	sabien
Preterite	sabí /	sabérem /
	vaig saber	vam saber
	saberes /	sabéreu /
	vas saber	vau saber
	sabé /	saberen /
	va saber	van saber
Future	sabré	sabrem
	sabràs	sabreu
	sabrà	sabran
Imperative	—	sapiguem
	sàpigues	sapigueu
	sàpiga	sàpiguen
Gerund	sabent	

sentir to feel; to hear

Present	sento	sentim
	sents	sentiu
	sent	senten

Imperfect	sentia	sentíem
	senties	sentíeu
	sentia	sentien

Preterite	sentí /	sentírem /
	vaig sentir	vam sentir
	sentires /	sentíreu /
	vas sentir	vau sentir
	sentí /	sentiren /
	va sentir	van sentir

Future	sentiré	sentirem
	sentiràs	sentireu
	sentirà	sentiran

Imperative	—	sentim
	sent	sentiu
	senti	sentin

Gerund	sentint

ser / ésser to be

Present	sóc	som
	ets	sou
	és	són

Imperfect	era	érem
	eres	éreu
	era	eren

Preterite	fui / vaig ésser	fórem / vam ésser
	fores / vas ésser	fóreu / vau ésser
	fou / va ésser	foren / van ésser

Future	seré	serem
	seràs	sereu
	serà	seran

Imperative	—	siguem
	sigues	sigueu
	sigui	siguin
Gerund	sent / essent	

servir to serve

Present	serveixo	servim
	serveixes	serviu
	serveix	serveixen
Imperfect	servia	servíem
	servies	servíeu
	servia	servien
Preterite	serví /	servírem /
	vaig servir	vam servir
	servires /	servíreu /
	vas servir	vau servir
	serví /	serviren /
	va servir	van servir
Future	serviré	servirem
	serviràs	servireu
	servirà	serviran
Imperative	—	servim
	serveix	serviu
	serveixi	serveixin
Gerund	servint	

tenir to have

Present	tinc	tenim
	tens	teniu
	té	tenen
Imperfect	tenia	teníem
	tenies	teníeu
	tenia	tenien

Preterite	tinguí /	tinguérem /
	vaig tenir	vam tenir
	tingueres /	tinguéreu /
	vas tenir	vau tenir
	tingué /	tingueren /
	va tenir	van tenir
Future	tindré	tindrem
	tindràs	tindreu
	tindrà	tindran
Imperative	—	tinguem
	té, tingues	teniu, tingueu
	tingui	tinguin
Gerund	tenint	

usar to use

Present	uso	usem
	uses	useu
	usa	usen
Imperfect	usava	usàvem
	usaves	usàveu
	usava	usaven
Preterite	usí / vaig usar	usàrem /
		vam usar
	usares /	usàreu /
	vas usar	vau usar
	usà / va usar	usaren / van usar
Future	usaré	usarem
	usaràs	usareu
	usarà	usaran
Imperative	—	usem
	usa	useu
	usi	usin
Gerund	usant	

vendre to sell

Present	venc	venem
	vens	veneu
	ven	venen
Imperfect	venia	veníem
	venies	veníeu
	venia	venien
Preterite	venguí /	venguérem /
	vaig vendre	vam vendre
	vengueres /	venguéreu /
	vas vendre	vau vendre
	vengué /	vengueren /
	va vendre	van vendre
Future	vendré	vendrem
	vendràs	vendreu
	vendrà	vendran
Imperative	—	venguem
	ven	veneu
	vengui	venguin
Gerund	venent	

venir to come

Present	vinc	venim
	véns	veniu
	ve	vénen
Imperfect	venia	veníem
	venies	veníeu
	venia	venien
Preterite	vinguí /	vinguérem /
	vaig venir	vam venir
	vingueres /	vinguéreu /
	vas venir	vau venir
	vingué /	vingueren /
	va venir	van venir

Future	vindré	vindrem
	vindràs	vindreu
	vindrà	vindran
Imperative	—	vinguem
	vina	veniu
	vingui	vinguin
Gerund	venint	

veure to see

Present	veig	veiem
	veus	veieu
	veu	veuen
Imperfect	veia	vèiem
	veies	vèieu
	veia	veien
Preterite	viu /	veiérem /
	vaig veure	vam veure
	veieres /	veiéreu /
	vas veure	vau veure
	veié /	veieren /
	va veure	van veure
Future	veuré	veurem
	veuràs	veureu
	veurà	veuran
Imperative	—	vegem
	veges, ves	vegeu, veieu
	vegi	vegin
Gerund	veient	

voler to want

Present	vull	volem
	vols	voleu
	vol	volen

Imperfect	volia	volíem
	volies	volíeu
	volia	volien
Preterite	volguí /	volguérem /
	vaig voler	vam voler
	volgueres /	volguéreu /
	vas voler	vau voler
	volgué /	volgueren /
	va voler	van voler
Future	voldré	voldrem
	voldràs	voldreu
	voldrà	voldran
Imperative	—	vulguem
	vulgues	vulgueu
	vulgui	vulguin
Gerund	volent	

www.ingramcontent.com/pod-product-compliance
Lightning Source LLC
Jackson TN
JSHW011400130125
77033JS00023B/760